SHAKESPEARE'S PROSE

Shakespeare's Prose

By

Milton Crane

THE UNIVERSITY OF CHICAGO PRESS
CHICAGO · ILLINOIS
CAMBRIDGE: AT THE UNIVERSITY PRESS

The University of Chicago Press, Chicago 37
Cambridge University Press, London, N.W. 1, England
W. J. Gage & Co., Limited, Toronto 2B, Canada

C

Printed in Germany by J. J. Augustin, Glückstadt

TO
OSCAR JAMES CAMPBELL

PREFACE

The purpose of this book is to examine in some detail the use which Shakespeare made of prose in his plays. It is clear that a consideration of Shakespeare's prose necessarily involves the most profound problems of the structure and texture of the plays, for it is impossible to treat the prose apart from the verse, or the prose scenes apart from the verse scenes. Prose is but one of the elements in the plays and must be understood in the context of the plays, not *in vacuo*. A study of the prose, therefore, will ultimately have value only insofar as it directs the reader's attention to larger critical questions concerning Shakespeare's art and technique. It is in that hope alone that any man dares to add a single item to the critical bibliography of Shakespeare.

Mr. Richard David will find in the present book the spiritual descendant of his brief but illuminating essay on Shakespeare, *The Janus of Poets*. Professor Mark Van Doren originally suggested the idea, as he has suggested so many. The late Professor Theodore Spencer supervised the preparation of a first version as a dissertation at Harvard University. The late Professor George Lyman Kittredge and Mr. Harley Granville-Barker generously supplied advice and information in memorable conversations. Both the book and its author owe most of all, however, to the expert scholarship and profound critical insight of Professor Oscar James Campbell.

M. C.

Chicago, Illinois
January, 1951

TABLE OF CONTENTS

I

Shakespeare and Dramatic Prose

> *Jaques.* Nay, then, God b'wi' you,
> an you talk in blank verse!

Shakespeare's prose is beyond question the finest body of prose by a writer in English. The idea may at first appear strange; one grants that Shakespeare wrote prose, but one may hesitate to admit him to the company of prose writers, for, after all, he wrote dramatic prose. Any roster of artists in English prose is likely, however, to include not only novelists but historians, biographers, critics, philosophers, scientists, and theologians—and who would take it upon himself to exclude Congreve or Shaw? And Shakespeare leads them all. His prose is the richest and most various in the language; it draws its greatest strength and suppleness from the fact that it was written to be spoken by characters in plays. At its best, it contributes enormously to the depiction of personality, and it is an indispensable element in the creation of atmosphere. And even at its least interesting, as in the journeyman scenes of exposition, it is less obtrusive than the purely utilitarian verse, which can range from neutral to downright distressing.

It was Shakespeare's good fortune to write prose in an age which made no sharp stylistic demarcation between literary dramatic prose and the prose of common speech. Like John Middleton Synge, Shakespeare was free to draw on the prose of the city and hamlet for its vigorous natural rhythms and its unconscious beauty. We may imagine, with Bernard

Shaw in *The Dark Lady of the Sonnets*, that Shakespeare assiduously jotted down for later use the felicitous phrases of beefeaters; but whether or not we commit ourselves to such a theory, we can hardly fail to recognize, in the excellence of Falstaff's prose, Shakespeare's delighted awareness of Elizabethan speech. The racy language of the London streets figured significantly in the development of the finest dramatic prose that our language—or any other—has ever known.

Prose has for so long been the unquestioned medium for English drama that one conceives only with difficulty of a truly popular drama in verse, or in a combination of prose and verse. Yet the ascendance of dramatic prose is a relatively recent phenomenon, as the history of European drama demonstrates; prose first found its way into the verse play by fulfilling certain functions which dramatists were for some reason unwilling to delegate to verse. This development appeared in a highly concentrated form in the Elizabethan and Jacobean drama, and above all in the plays of Shakespeare. For he, more than any other playwright, successfully combined the media of prose and verse. He was, moreover, fully aware of his achievement: his brilliant blending and contrasting of the two forms should alone serve to confute that curious scholar who suggested that Shakespeare actually wrote only verse and incomprehensibly permitted almost forty per cent of it to be printed as prose.

The beginnings of English dramatic prose are veiled in obscurity; in the Elizabethan drama before Shakespeare, Lyly and Marlowe stood almost alone in regarding prose as useful for any purpose more elevated than the speech of clowns. The most typical conventional uses of prose—for letters and proclamations, madness, and comic matter—were well established by 1590. They were grounded in a more or less conscious awareness of the nature of poetic drama, and also, perhaps, in simple imitation of life. Proclamations, for example, were known from common experience to be written in prose; and only a very imaginative dramatist would have written a proclamation in verse. In a verse play, a letter or a proclamation is an intrusion from the world without, and the symbolic representation of such intrusion is heightened by that marked formal differentiation which the use of prose supplies. In the same way, the verse play used prose to represent madness or derangement; the normal mode of speech in the play was verse, and the introduction of prose signified the failure of a character to conform with the prevailing mode of his world. This doubly satisfying convention was one of the most artful developed by the English drama. For the madman is expressly marked off from other characters by his prose, and his disintegration is forcefully represented by his speaking irregular prose while the other characters continue to speak regular verse. Comedy, in the earlier drama, is also little more than a fall into absurdity from the heights of the serious verse action, a fall which could be appropriately mirrored in prose.

These conventions Shakespeare knew, and, after his fashion, utilized. He rarely violated them, for he must have realized how solidly they were based in the very structure of the prose-verse play. But his development of the conventions was extremely subtle and skillful; the simple division of verse for serious matter and prose for comic matter which prevailed in the pre-Shakespearean drama is meaningless when applied to *Hamlet* or *King Lear*. The several conventions of the pre-Shakespearean drama ceased to exist as discrete rules and were assimilated into the structure of the Shakespearean play.

For the use of prose in the mature Elizabethan drama may be considered, in its totality, a single convention. The meaning of this convention is the establishment of dramatic contrast between the prose and the dominant verse. Shakespeare and his fellow dramatists all employed prose according to their tastes and abilities, and a knowledge and evaluation of their individual achievements is essential if one is to make a comprehensive judgment of Shakespeare's practice. Shakepeare's success is great not only because of his superior technical invention, but because of the extraordinary beauty and richness of his prose. In the works of many of his fellows, prose remained always an inferior medium, something that would serve for clowns but that was hardly worthy of a dramatist's best efforts. Shakespeare evidently held prose in no such contempt, or he could hardly have put so much art into the prose of Hamlet and Falstaff. He already had a vigorous and brilliant prose style when he was still far from his peak as a verse writer. George H. W. Rylands has even maintained that Shakespeare developed his mature verse style through his study of dramatic prose.[1] The colloquial and realistic quality of much of Shakespeare's finest verse may well owe not a little to his work in prose.

Realism, wit, common sense make up the quintessence of comedy, and the characteristic idiom of comedy is prose— "common speech artistically heightened." Without prose, Shakespearean comedy would be unthinkable; and, from the start, Shakespeare's progress as a writer of dramatic prose can be best charted in his comedies. One encounters difficulties, to be sure: the contrast of prose and verse is characteristically more striking in tragedy than in comedy, for the opposition of the two media may be blurred in comedy by the sheer volume of prose and by the relatively greater fluidity of both prose and verse. The typical balance of prose and verse may actually be reversed, as in *Much Ado About Nothing*, in which it is the verse that is contrasted with the dominant prose. The element of contrast remains basic and omnipresent, nevertheless, although it may exist in combination with such factors as the delineation of character in prose. Falstaff is surely the most striking example of characterization in prose. He speaks verse only to mock it, for it is totally foreign to his personality. In the two parts of *King Henry IV*, the simple and familiar contrast of prose and verse within a single scene is expanded to a larger conflict between Falstaff's world of prose realism and the world of verse and nobility, whose ideals and whose very language he derides.

Prose is also used effectively in the characterization of the tragic hero. Hamlet, for example, is created in both prose and verse partly in order to symbolize his inner conflict. After his initial encounter with the Ghost, Hamlet can reveal himself in verse only in soliloquy or to Horatio; Hamlet, at grips with a hostile and dangerous court, communicates with it in prose. His chief motive for speaking prose is to feign madness, but it is not his sole motive: Hamlet with Rosencrantz and Guildenstern satirizes the world, maintains a suspicious reserve, admits the fact of his melancholy but conceals its cause; Hamlet with the Players anatomizes the art of acting; Hamlet with Horatio and the Gravediggers jests about mortality and moralizes on the skull of Yorick — all in prose.

Within the individual scene, both in comedy and in tragedy, prose may be contrasted with verse in at least two ways. Parts of the same scene may be set off against one another, or a character may be opposed to the prevailing tone of the scene in which he figures. Cleopatra's dialogue with the clown, in the final scene of *Antony and Cleopatra*, stands significantly between Cleopatra's preparations for death and the very spectacle of that death. Similarly, the Porter's prose monologue in *Macbeth* follows the verse conversation of Macbeth and Lady Macbeth after the murder of Duncan, and is itself followed by the dialogue in verse attendant on the discovery of the murder. On the other hand, the isolation of a character by the use of prose appears strikingly in all the scenes of *Troilus and Cressida* that show Thersites at loggerheads with the Greek heroes. Virtually all satirical commentators in the plays, for that matter, speak prose, as an emblem of their separation from the action that they criticize. Prose performs a parallel function for Hamlet in the play-scene; he alone among the spectators annotates the action of *The Murder of Gonzago* with his edged comments in prose. Verse as well as prose may single out an individual in a group: Lord Say, in the hands of Jack Cade's men in *2 Henry VI*, defends himself in a verse which conflicts nobly with the revolutionists' disjointed and scurrilous prose.

In the present study I have considered those histories of Shakespeare whose prose is preponderantly comic together with the comedies, and those histories whose prose is chiefly serious together with the tragedies. Within these categories, the plays are examined chronologically. In justification of this division, it should be pointed out that the development of prose in the tragedies and that in the comedies are not parallel. That a difference should exist is entirely understandable, for the large proportion of prose in even the earliest comedies must have invited or required greater inventive efforts in prose than did the substantially smaller quantities of prose in the early tragedies and histories. An examination of *Love's Labour's Lost* and *Titus Andronicus* reveals that the prose in the early comedy is quite sophisticated and mature, whereas that in the early tragedy is of the most primitive. The application of a rigidly chronological method would portray a wholly incredible and misleading development. Within the categories I have employed, a consistent development can be traced under relatively constant conditions. The progress from comedy to comedy and from tragedy to tragedy, although occasionally blurred by gaps of time, is on the whole clearly discernible.

In attempting to define the function of prose in the Shakespearean play, one must guard against imposing purely theoretical rules that cannot survive a pragmatic test. Most earlier writers on Shakespeare's prose either propounded broad and vague theories, which obliged them to rationalize or ignore the numerous exceptions in which Shakespeare abounds, or offered fantastically exhaustive lists of specific explanations. Thus, Henry Sharpe was obliged to establish as a rule that "Ladies speak prose when alone, or nearly alone, with female relations ..."[2] The value of such theorizing is at best doubtful. Whether Shakespeare's intention can be divined at all is open to question, of course; but it is effectively clear that any attempt to explain his practice must be specific enough to endure application, and not so minute as to become preposterous.

It seems ironical that Shakespeare, the greatest master of the prose-verse drama, should bear much of the responsibility for the decline of the form in which he wrote his masterpieces. For the dramatic prose which Shakespeare and his colleagues so richly developed offered a valuable dramatic idiom for the growing realism of the Elizabethan and Jacobean drama, as well as for the comedy of manners. The encroachments of prose produced such notable all-prose plays as Jonson's *Bartholomew Fair*, one of the great realistic comedies, and Jonson's *Epicœne*, which was inferior in neither elegance nor polish to the Restoration comedy it helped to launch. Naturalism need not always seek its expression in prose, nor symbolism in verse, as both the Elizabethans and we can bear witness: who would call Hotspur's verse less naturalistic than the prose of Lyly's *Endimion?* The Elizabethans were learning that the form of *The Spanish Tragedie* was hopelessly inappropriate for the matter of *The*

Shoemaker's Holiday. But their new art form cost them the prose-verse drama.

Other influences, to be sure, contributed to the decline of the older form. The break in English dramatic tradition that came with the closing of the theatres in 1642; the diversion of interest to non-dramatic poetry in Stuart and Commonwealth England; and the very character of Restoration drama all helped to undermine the prose-verse play. And yet one finds even in Wycherley's *The Plain Dealer* the curious verse soliloquies of the passionate Fidelia, indicating that vestigial elements of the Elizabethan tradition lived on. On the one hand, the realism of Restoration comedy found a perfect medium in the prose it had inherited from Jonson and Dekker; on the other, the heroic play of the Restoration continued to restrict prose to comic scenes. Experiments in the combined use of blank verse, rhymed verse, and prose, as in Etherege's *Love in a Tub*, were not unknown. But a basic self-consciousness vitiated all the attempts of the Restoration to revive the mixed form, and subsequent efforts have been no more successful. T. S. Eliot's *Murder in the Cathedral* and Maxwell Anderson's imitations of Elizabethan drama have not heralded a popular revival of the poetic drama; nor has prose proved an unsatisfactory medium for symbolist drama. The problem can obviously not be resolved in merely formal terms; only a great conception can find great expression in either prose or verse.

II

English Dramatic Prose before Shakespeare

Prose was well established in the Elizabethan drama long before Shakespeare came to London. In order to understand the background against which Shakespeare worked during his entire career, it will be necessary to examine in some detail the use of prose made by his most significant predecessors and fellow-playwrights. An appreciation of their reasons for introducing dramatic prose into their plays will permit a fairer assessment of Shakespeare's indebtedness to accepted convention and of his innovations. The earliest appearances of prose in the drama, in George Gascoigne's translation of Ariosto's *I Suppositi* and in Henry Medwall's *Nature*, are not strictly germane to this study. Gascoigne may have chosen prose for his translation because he deemed it more appropriate to the matter of the play or to his artistic purpose than verse; but, in the absence of such information, his prose version can play no part in the history of dramatic prose in English.

Among Shakespeare's predecessors, Lyly, Marlowe, and Kyd were most imaginative in their use of prose, and their plays will be treated here in some detail as representative of the pre-Shakespearean drama. Other playwrights will be considered more briefly.

1. *Lyly*

R. Warwick Bond, in his edition of Lyly's works, sums up in the following words Lyly's contribution to English dramatic prose:

[Lyly] resolved to throw the whole of his matter into prose, prose which he made now serious and dignified, now bright and witty, but such as always gave the sense of selective skill and controlling power. He asserted his freedom from mechanical slavery, but only that he might better obey the higher laws of dramatic and literary effect. He was not the first dramatist to use prose; but he was the first to demonstrate, by persistent and successful use of it, its claim to be the received vehicle for English comedy.[3]

This statement of Lyly's achievement is unexceptionable, but surely Mr. Bond's explanation of Lyly's decision to adopt prose is incomplete. A study of the plays reveals the dramatist's steadily developing maturity of technique, but can hardly make one feel that when Lyly forsook the novel for the drama he was already a seasoned master of his new art.

Euphues, or the Anatomy of Wit, was published in 1578, *Euphues and his England* in 1580; and although *Campaspe,* Lyly's first play, was not published until 1584, Bond presents evidence to show that it was written either before or concurrently with the second novel. *Campaspe* is, therefore, the work of a man who became overnight the darling of Elizabeth's court, the chief exponent in English of a most extraordinary and ornate prose style. For some reason (and modern parallels may here prove instructive) Lyly determined to try his hand at a play. His subject differed radically from the familiar matter of the English play, and in its essentials recalled the courtly subjects of the interminable conversations of *Euphues.*

Lyly's great reputation, as may be seen from the echoes of his work in the writings of his contemporaries and successors, was based not on his narrative or philosophical gifts but on his unique style. It was entirely natural, therefore, for him to wish to capitalize on his fame and to extend it in his new medium. The slightest effort to employ the Euphuistic style in verse must have shown him at once the futility of such a hope; and, Bond to the contrary, Lyly was in any case no great poet. To say, then, that Lyly was moved to adopt prose as the best medium for his plays because it afforded him an unexampled opportunity to display the style for which he was celebrated is not too crass an interpretation. Lyly soon discovered, however, that Euphuism could be displayed more effectively in a novel than in a play. The Euphues-novels are hardly novels by modern standards; plot and characterization are almost totally absent, and the reader's attention and interest are engaged (if at all) only by the long and elaborate speeches. But the drama is a far more demanding form, and Lyly speedily found himself making compromises he had perhaps not envisaged. G. C. Child, in a chart reprinted by Bond,[4] demonstrates statistically the decline of the Euphuistic figures in Lyly's plays. The numbers are striking; *Midas* (1592) and *Mother Bombie* (1594), two of Lyly's last plays, show an especially remarkable diminution of Euphuistic rhetorical devices.

Whatever may have been Lyly's original motive for choosing prose as his vehicle, his achievement as a dramatist in prose is unquestionable. His light romantic comedy is matched only by Shakespeare's; and he adapted with skill and fine dramatic sense the amorous dialogues and debates of his novels. His prose necessarily displays extreme artificiality, and often uses the devices of both prose and verse. In *Gallathea*, for example, the maiden Hæbe is to be sacrificed to a monster, and bewails her fate in nicely articulated periods. Her speech is divided into three stanzas, which employ refrains, as well as the more familiar Euphuistic devices of alliteration (simple and transverse) and repetition.

Myserable and accursed *Hœbe*, that beeing neither faire nor fortunate, thou shouldest be thought most happy and beautifull. Curse thy birth, thy lyfe, thy death, beeing borne to liue in danger, and hauing liude, to die by deceit. Art thou the sacrifice to appease *Neptune*, and

satisfie the custome, the bloodie custom, ordained for the safetie of thy
Country? I *Hœbe*, poore *Hœbe*, men will haue it so, whose forces com-
maund our weake natures; nay the Gods will haue it so, whose powers
dally with our purposes. The Egiptians neuer cut their Dates from the
tree, because they are so fresh and greene. It is thought wickednes to
pul Roses from the stalkes in the Garden of Palestine, for that they haue
so liuelie a redde: and who so cutteth the incense Tree in Arabia before
it fal, committeth sacriledge.

Shall it onely be lawfull amongst vs in the prime of youth, and pride
of beautie, to destroy both youth and beautie: and what was honoured
in fruits and flowres as a vertue, to violate in a virgine as a vice? But,
alas! destenie alloweth no dispute; die *Hœbe*, *Hœbe* die! wofull *Hœbe!*
and onely accursed *Hœbe!* Farewell the sweete delights of life, and
welcome nowe the bitter pangs of death. Farewell you chast virgins,
whose thoughts are diuine, whose faces faire, whose fortunes are
agreeable to your affections, enioy and long enioy the pleasure of your
curled locks, the amiablenesse of your wished lookes, the sweetnes of
your tuned voices, the content of your inwarde thoughts, the pompe
of your outward showes: onely *Hœbe* biddeth farewell to all the ioyes
that she conceiued, and you hope for, that shee possessed, and you
shall; fare-well the pompe of Princes Courts, whose roofes are imbosst
with gold, and whose pauements are decked with faire Ladies, where
the daies are spent in sweet delights, the nights in pleasant dreames,
where chastitie honoreth affections and commaundeth, yeeldeth to desire
and conquereth.

Fare-well the Soueraigne of all vertue, and Goddesse of all virgins,
Diana, whose perfections are impossible to be numbred, and therefore
infinite, neuer to be matched, and therefore immortall. Fare-well
sweet Parents, yet, to be mine, vnfortunate Parents! Howe blessed,
had you beene in barrennes! how happy had I been, if I had not beene!
Farewell life, vaine life, wretched life, whose sorrowes are long, whose
ende doubtfull, whose miseries certaine, whose hopes innumerable,
whose feares intollerable. Come death, and welcome death whom nature cannot resist, because necessity ruleth, nor deferre because destenie
hasteth. Come *Agar* thou vnsatiable Monster of Maidens blood, &
deuourer of beauties bowels, glut thy selfe till thou surfet, & let my
life and thine. Teare these tender ioynts wyth thy greedie iawes, these
yellow lockes with thy black feete, this faire face with thy foule teeth.
Why abatest thou thy wonted swiftnesse? I am faire, I am a virgine, I
am readie. Come *Agar* thou horrible monster, & farewell world thou
viler Monster.[5]

There are Euphuistic figures in this speech as extravagant as any in the novels; mark the alliteration of "and what was honoured in fruits and flowres as a vertue, to violate in a virgine as a vice." And the structure of the speech itself is quite rigid; the paragraphs have a stanzaic organization. A theme is stated in the middle of a paragraph, and reiterated with new force and more personal application in the following paragraph. Thus the "unnatural natural history" of the Egyptian date-tree, the Palestinian rose-bush, and the Arabian incense-tree lead directly to the bitter complaint against the wanton destruction of youth; and the farewell to life and pomp becomes the principal theme of the last paragraph after it has been introduced in more general terms in the second paragraph.

For all the pathos of Hæbe's situation and the sincerity which from time to time breaks through the formal structure of the speech, the net effect is that of a set piece. This impression is ironically heightened by Hæbe's last speech of the scene, after the monster has rejected her:

Fortunate *Hæbe*, howe shalt thou expresse thy ioyes? Nay vnhappy girle that art not the fairest. Had it not been better for thee to haue died with fame, then to liue with dishonour, to haue preferred the safetie of thy Countrey and rarenesse of thy beautie, before sweetnes of life, & vanity of the world? But alas! desteny would not haue it so, desteny could not, for it asketh the beautifullest. I would *Hæbe* thou hadst been beautifullest.[6]

Lyly's psychological penetration is delightful, but the immediate dramatic effect of the speech is marred by the elaborate structure of the prose.

It has already been suggested that chief among Lyly's reasons for using prose was the desire to exploit most effectively the style which he had made famous. Lyly was not, of course, incapable of writing any other kind of dramatic prose; *Mother Bombie*, which Bond sets sixth in his chronological order of Lyly's plays, stands as Lyly's unique work in realistic prose and has the fewest Euphuistic figures of all the plays. Its prose is largely simple, straightforward, and lively; the speeches are short. Lyly seems to have allowed his matter to govern his manner, in refusing to couch his Terentian plot in the style of *Campaspe*.

Lyly's one verse play, *The Woman in the Moone* (1597), introduces prose sparingly but significantly. One character, the clown Gunophilus, speaks prose quite regularly after he assumes an important part in the intrigue and becomes the comic element of the play. He offers an ironic commentary on the other characters, particularly in the scenes which show Pandora, under the sway of Venus, accepting the clown as a lover.

Pandora herself speaks prose briefly at the middle of V, i, when she has fallen under the influence of Luna and gone mad. Her first mad speeches are interrupted by the entrance of Stesias, who enumerates the charms of his bower. She bursts out in reply: "Streames with pearles? birdes with golden feathers? Musk flyes, and amber berries? white Squirrels, And singing Popiniayes? a boat of deare skins? Come, Ile goe! Ile go!"[7] Gunophilus is moved to comment:

> I was nere in loue with her till now. O absolute *Pandora!* because folish, for folly is womens perfection. To talke Idely, to loke wildly, to laugh at euery breath and play with a feather, is that would make a Stoyke in loue, yea, thou they selfe,
>
> *O Marce fili annum iam audientem Cratippum idque Athenis.*
>
> Grauity in a woman is like to a gray beard vpon a breaching boies chinne, which a good Scholemaister would cause to be clipt, and the wise husband to be avoyded.[8]

The other instances in which prose is used are trifling: Learchus reads and moralizes upon a letter in IV, i, and Stesias falls briefly into prose in the ecstasy of his rage at the end of Act IV.

The Woman in the Moone shows Lyly following estab-lished conventions in permitting a clown and a madwoman to speak most of the little prose in the play. The difficulty of dating the play makes it impossible to assess influences exercised on or by the play. Since it cannot, however, much antedate Bond's suggested date of 1590, it is clear that Lyly had ample time to become familiar with the conventional dramatic use of prose. *Tamburlaine* had already been played and published, to look no further; and it would be absurd to suppose that Lyly had to learn such conventions from Marlowe. Bond is less certain: "Following Marlowe's example Lyly had, too, the sense to perceive, not only that comic matter hardly admits of verse, but that its effect may be greatly enhanced by a transition to prose, the vehicle of common sense."[9] Bond is on safer ground when he makes Shakespeare Lyly's debtor for "the example of a prose-dia-logue" and adduces more specific evidence of Shakespeare's use of Lyly. For it is not to be doubted that Shakespeare looked to Lyly as the master of light and graceful prose dia-logue. Lyly's influence may be seen in *Love's Labour's Lost* and in *As You Like It*, and less markedly, in almost all Shakespeare's comedies. Some of the comic monologues in *Mother Bombie* find an echo in the speeches of Launce and of the other Shakespearean clowns whose parts are associated with the great comedian Will Kempe.

Lyly was unquestionably the first playwright in English to realize and exploit the possibilities of using prose extensively in drama; although his primary motives for employing prose may have been undramatic, the results are admirable. His single play in the mixed form tells us but little of the problems of the prose-verse dramatist, but proves him to have been aware of the practice of his contemporaries.

2. *Marlowe*

Marlowe's prose is especially useful as a touchstone for the study of Shakespeare's prose, for Marlowe was decidedly not a playwright who found in prose a natural and satisfying medium. He expressed himself best in verse of a surpassing beauty, but a verse which emphasized his primary concern with superhuman rather than human problems. The greatest bulk of his prose is in *Dr. Faustus* and *The Jew of Malta*; in the former, the prose is used for the comic scenes which offer so curious a commentary on the serious action of the play, and, in the latter, the strange jumble of prose and verse emphasizes the unevenness and diffuseness of the entire play.

The prose in *Tamburlaine, Part I*, (1590), centers entirely on the plot of the captive Bajazeth. An exchange of curses between Tamburlaine and Bajazeth in IV, iv, is in both verse and prose, prose being reserved for the episode in which Tamburlaine and his lieutenants contemptuously mock their prisoner. When the curses are in the more common high astounding terms, they return to verse. Later in the scene a very formal prose is introduced for the crowning of the lieutenants.

Most interesting of all is Zabina's mad speech in V, ii, the first instance of mad prose in Elizabethan drama.

> What do mine eies behold, my husband dead?
> His Skul al riuin in twain, his braines dasht out?
> The braines of *Baiazeth*, my Lord and Soueraigne?
> O *Baiazeth*, my husband and my Lord,
>
> O *Baiazet*, O Turk, O Emperor, giue him his liquor?
> Not I, bring milk and fire, and my blood I bring him againe, teare me in peeces, giue me the sworde with a ball of wildefire vpon it. Downe with him, downe with him. Goe to my child, away, away, away. Ah, saue that Infant, saue him, saue him. I, euen, I, speake to her, the Sun was downe.
> Streamers white, Red, Blacke, here, here, here. Fling the meat in his face. *Tamburlaine*, *Tamburlaine*, Let the souldiers be buried. Hel, death, *Tamburlain*. Hell, make ready my Coch, my chaire, my iewels, I come, I come, I come.[10]

The abrupt change from verse to prose is shocking and impressive. The Elizabethan drama can offer relatively few examples of a mixture of forms within the framework of a single speech—Lear's tirade on the inconstancy of woman is doubtless the most memorable—and the transformation of Zabina's speech admirably reflects the gradual darkening of her mind.

The symbolic significance and value of using prose to indicate the madness of the speaker appear strikingly here. In the prose-verse play, verse is the staple form; a character who, because of mental derangement, cannot maintain his accustomed position, undergoes a symbolic change in discarding verse for prose. And, in the rare mixed speeches, a single subject may be treated both sanely and insanely. Thus, Zabina begins a ranting speech in the old manner, which she sustains until "O *Baiazeth*, my husband and my Lord," at which point the form breaks down and the apostrophe disintegrates with the repetition of Bajazeth's name. For repetition itself is, in a sense, the keynote of this technique of representing insanity. The disorganized mind seizes on an idea and worries it, then as quickly rejects it for another. Zabina's rapid recapitulation of all her recent miseries will find an echo in Lady Macbeth's sleepwalking scene.

The commonest unit of repetition is the group of three, although Zabina twice uses doublets: "Downe with him, downe with him" and "*Tamburlaine, Tamburlaine.*" Sometimes the triplet rings changes on a single idea: "O *Baiazet*, O Turk, O Emperor," "Hel, death, *Tamburlain*," in which note the climactic effect of the progression; again, a single phrase is repeated with fearful intensity: "I come, I come, I come."

A logical connection joins the first part of the speech with the preceding action, permitting Zabina to proceed from the idea of bringing Bajazeth his liquor to the introduction

2

of milk and blood. But she wanders at once into remini-scenees of her child, the symbolic colored streamers of Tam-burlaine, and the tormenting of Bajazeth in his cage. In spite of the resemblance between this scene and Lady Macbeth's sleepwalking speeches, Zabina's is the far more mannered speech; her break with the rigidity of blank verse in fact exchanges one discipline for another.

Zabina's speech is "conventional," as Lady Macbeth's is not, although both obey a convention. Lady Macbeth reveals an unsuspected side of her character; Zabina has nothing new to reveal. Marlowe's characters not infrequently tell all that one needs to know about them within five minutes of their first entrance. Zabina's motives for grief, revenge, and suicide are all known before she ever begins to speak, and her speech in no way increases one's knowledge or under-standing of her. What she actually achieves is a sudden heightening of sympathy for her and for Bajazeth, both of whom have hitherto been quite as monstrous and unbeliev-able as their tormentor. And the modern reader, who comes to *Tamburlaine* with a knowledge of Shakespeare's plays, will find a singularly moving suggestion of Cleopatra's preparations for death in Zabina's last words: "Make ready my Coch, my chaire, my iewels . . ."

The influence of Marlowe's mad prose on later dramatists, and on Shakespeare in particular, can hardly be measured with accuracy. One must feel, however, that Shakespeare, in writing his elaborate psychological and formal treatments of madness, found a worthy precursor in Marlowe.

In *Tamburlaine, Part II*, prose is used first, with uncer-tain value, in the seduction of Almeda by Callapine. The traitor Almeda speaks prose, and inconsistently. He is later to reappear as a comic figure, and his prose in the first act may be a foreshadowing of his comic rôle.

In III, i, Orcanes speaks prose in crowning Callapine: a

speech which is largely a listing of the new emperor's theoretical possessions. This is another example of the formal prose which was observed in the scene of Tamburlaine's crowning of his lieutenants, in Part I. It is likewise the familiar, conventional prose of proclamations and other formal documents.

The other occurrences of prose in Part II—with the exception of the Messenger's announcement in V, iii—are all more or less comic, as in III, ii, where the little scourges of God clamor to be wounded by Tamburlaine, while Calyphas confesses his distaste for the sport. In III, v, Tamburlaine and Orcanes hurl insults at each other in verse. When Tamburlaine turns his attention to Callapine and later to Almeda, he drops into prose, which, from its content as well as from the changed mood of the situation, is clearly comic prose. And the comic conversation of Calyphas and Perdicas in IV, i, brings a return to prose. It is to be noted that in all the scenes in which prose is employed for comic purposes, the nobles speak it as freely as the Almedas. One finds no exact and clearcut divisions, and characters change media with almost excessive facility.

The insignificant quantities of prose in *Tamburlaine* may be explained by the comment of Marlowe's printer:

> I have (purposely) omitted and left out some fond and friuolous Iestures, digressing (and in my poore opinion) far vnmeet for the matter, which I thought, might seeme more tedious vnto the wise, than anyway els to be regarded, though (happly) they have bene of some vaine conceited fondlings greatly gaped at, what times they were shewed vpon the stage in their graced deformities: neuertheles now, to prooue a great disgrace to so honorable and stately a historie...[11]

Dr. Faustus (published 1604) and *The Jew of Malta* (published 1633) may suggest something of the nature of the missing comic scenes in the two parts of *Tamburlaine*. Like the Rafe-Robin scenes in *Dr. Faustus* and the Ithamore-

2*

Bellamira-Pilia-Borza plot in *The Jew of Malta*, they probably burlesqued the main notion of *Tamburlaine*. Indeed,
the comic sub-plot (if one may so exalt it) of Almeda in Part
II seems a survival of such comic action. And from this
evidence, as well as from Marlowe's other comic matter, we
may well assume that the lost scenes were in prose.

Although much of *Dr. Faustus*' prose is in familiar
patterns, some of it remains almost inexplicable. Thus there
are, on the one hand, the comic scenes of Rafe and Robin,
of Wagner and the Clown, which directly travesty Faustus'
thaumaturgy; but what is one to make of the scenes in which
Faustus and Mephistophilis themselves seem to mock the
high seriousness of Faustus' ideals? The cozening of the
horse-courser is unworthy of Faustus. And, later, prose is
used both for Mephistophilis' exposition of celestial mechanics and for the final tense meeting of Faustus and the scholars in the last scene but one of the play. Marlowe appears,
in *Dr. Faustus*, to have come to regard prose as a medium
not unworthy of him, and not merely as a vehicle for low
comedy. Zabina's speech, although explicable in terms of an
older convention, already points to a realization of the potentialities of prose, and *Dr. Faustus* carries on the development.

In the short scene between Wagner and the scholars
(lines 196–234), Wagner tells humorously of Faustus' interest in magic; and, after he leaves, the scholars continue
to discuss the distressing news in more sober terms. What
is curious and noteworthy is that the entire episode, and not
merely the first part, is in prose.

An instance demonstrating the nice care with which a
humorous interlude is set off in prose occurs in the long
scene of Faustus' compact with Mephistophilis (lines 433–
611). After the signing of the covenant, Mephistophilis answers Faustus' first questions, and the scene proceeds in

verse (the bond itself, of course, being in prose) until Faustus, in an extraordinary change of mood, debases the high philosophical tone of the dialogue and changes the medium to prose.

Mephistophilis. ... I am damnd, and am now in hell.

Faustus. How? now in hell? nay and this be hell, Ile willingly be damnd here: what walking, disputing, &c. But leauing off this, let me haue a wife, the fairest maid in *Germany*, for I am wanton and lasciuious, and can not liue without a wife.

Me. How, a wife? I prithee *Faustus* talke not of a wife.

Fau. Nay sweete *Mephistophilis* fetch me one, for I will haue one.

Me. Well thou wilt haue one, sit there till I come.

Ile fetch thee a wife in the diuels name. (*Exit*.)

Enter (Mephistophilis) with a diuell drest like a woman, with fier workes.

Me. Tel (me) Faustus, how dost thou like thy wife?

Fau. A plague on her for a hote whore.

Me. Tut Faustus,

Marriage is but a ceremoniall toy...[12]

The equilibrium of the scene is extremely unstable, and the inexplicable shifting between comic and grave matter is reflected in the unsystematic changes from verse to prose and again to verse. The most unstable element appears to be Faustus himself, who, in his eagerness to encompass at once all intellectual and sensual delight, succeeds only in reminding one of a child turned loose in a toy-shop. After Mephistophilis describes the contents of the magic book which he gives Faustus, the latter again drops suddenly into prose with a request for a sixteenth-century *Encyclopedia Britannica;* he then denies, in a final comic interlude, that such a library as he now has can possibly exist.

The textual and dramatic problems suggested by this scene are not easily settled. Was Marlowe perhaps no longer confident that the simple division between comic and heroic or tragic scenes, the division which produced the most elementary distribution of prose and verse in the pre-Shakespearean drama, remained valid? These curious mixed scenes in *Dr. Faustus* may be a development of the simple comic scene, or may merely bear witness to the imperfect state of the text. The play, although apparently composed in 1588–89, was not published until 1604. This version and the texts of 1609 and 1611 differ considerably; and the editions of 1616 to 1631 are half as long again as the original edition.

Frederick S. Boas, in his edition of *Dr. Faustus*, suggests plausible reasons for attributing to Marlowe alone some of the prose scenes in the original version of the play; and, although he puts forward Samuel Rowley as Marlowe's probable collaborator on other prose scenes, he tacitly assumes that Marlowe was entirely aware of the existence of such scenes.[13] No more is known of the authorship of the additions to *Dr. Faustus*, which make their appearance in the editions from 1616 to 1663, and which are almost equally divided between verse and prose. Virtually all the prose appears in comic scenes; according to Tucker Brooke, "some of the comic matter, like that omitted by the publisher of *Tamburlaine* . . . represents the improvisation of the company's clown."[14]

The prose of *The Jew of Malta* is chiefly comic, centering around the plot of Ithamore, Bellamira, and Pilia-Borza. It is interesting to note that prose appears only twice in the first two acts, that is, before the plot and the character of Barabas have been completely debased. These prose passages occur in the reading of the announcement concerning the tribute levy and in the scene of Ithamore's purchase: a conventional usage and a comic one, respectively.

Barabas himself generally speaks verse. In this connection, Marlowe observes, in III, ll. 1303–1419, a curious and primitive prose-verse division which Shakespeare is later to employ to great advantage. In the conversation between Barabas and Ithamore, the former speaks verse throughout, while the latter speaks verse before the scene's tone is altered, and prose afterwards, disregarding his master's use of verse. Ithamore's change of medium is dependent upon Barabas' change of mood; at first, Barabas is moved to fury and almost to grief by the news of Abigail's second conversion, and Ithamore's longest speech (one of three lines) is a reaffirmation of his loyalty to Barabas. After Ithamore's second entrance, when he brings the pot with which he is to poison Abigail, the conversation remains on a purely practical level; a decision has been made, there is no occasion for further heroics, and Ithamore jokes pleasantly about his new task.

In view of the fact that Barabas ordinarily speaks verse, his use of prose in the scene with Ithamore, Pilia-Borza, and Bellamira (IV, 1950–2001) is of peculiar interest. Barabas comes disguised as a French musician, speaking a broken English prose with asides in prose and verse. Here, clearly, prose is used as part of the disguise, as in Shakespeare (compare the scene of King Henry and Michael Williams in *Henry V*). Barabas comes down to the comedians' level and speaks prose as they do.

Barabas' verse makes it difficult, from a purely technical viewpoint, to consider him merely as a monstrous and grotesque clown. Even Shylock speaks more prose than Barabas, although Shylock is obviously a more grave and serious figure than Barabas.

It is obviously difficult to make any final statement about Marlowe's contribution to the development of dramatic prose, for his total output was very limited; although within the framework of his surviving plays there is comparatively little prose, the suspicion remains that Marlowe may have written more than has survived. Marlowe illustrates all the conventional prose uses of the early Elizabethan drama, and his work makes possible a clearer understanding of these conventions. His use of prose is in the main fairly primitive; he shows no great originality in using it to produce dramatic effects, nor is the prose itself highly distinguished. On occasion, however, it is capable of flexibility and vigor, as in these speeches of Pilia-Borza and Ithamore from *The Jew of Malta*:

> *Pilia-Borza.* (I met [Ithamore]) within 40 foot of the Gallowes conning his neck-verse I take it, looking of a Fryars Execution, whom I saluted with an old hempen prouerb, *Hodie tibi, cras mihi*, and so I left him to the mercy of the Hangman: but the Exercise being done, see where he comes.
>
> *Ithamore.* I neuer knew a man take his death so patiently as this Fryar; he was ready to leape off o're the halter was about his necke; and when the Hangman had put on his Hempen Tippet, he made such haste to his prayers, as if hee had had another Cure to serue; well, goe whither he will, I'le be none of his followers in haste: And now I thinke on't, going to the execution, a fellow met me with a muschatoes like a Rauens wing, and a Dagger with a hilt like a warming-pan, and he gaue me a letter from one Madam *Bellamira*, saluting me in such sort as if he had meant to make cleane my Boots with his lips; the effect was, that I should come to her house. I wonder what the reason is. It may be she sees more in me than I can find in my selfe: for she writes further, that she loues me euer since she saw me, and who would not requite such loue? here's her house, and here she comes, and now would I were gone, I am not worthy to looke vpon her.[15]

This is not to be compared with the prose of a Touchstone or a Falstaff; but it is not much inferior to that of Launce. It is certainly a far cry from the vaudeville of Rafe and Robin.

In a sense, what must be said of Marlowe's prose is intimately linked with what must be said of Marlowe in general: he developed and perpetuated many elements of the English drama as he found it, he made striking innovations, but the brevity of his life prevented him from attaining the full maturity at which his short career and his few brilliant plays hint.

3. *Kyd*

Prose occurs twice in the original text of Kyd's *The Spanish Tragedie* (published 1594), and once in the later additions. The many interesting differences which are to be noted between Kyd's text and the additions are to some degree reflected in the choice of medium. It is possible, although not entirely satisfactory, to explain the use of prose in each instance in terms of conventional usage, but an interpretation in terms of convention alone may ultimately reveal that these conventions are an expression of a larger dramatic relation between prose and verse.

The first appearance of prose is a quasi-humorous monologue in III, v, which falls as naturally into prose as do the speeches of Launce or Launcelot Gobbo. It happens also to be an interlude between two highly dramatic scenes. The latter scene, III, vi, contains a prose dialogue between Pedringano and the Hangman, itself set in a frame of intense and dramatic speeches by Hieronimo. The prose speeches have a gruesome humor, produced largely by the introduction of the false pardon, a more ironic theme than one is accustomed to find in such scenes. One's astonishment at finding Kyd dealing with such subtle niceties is in part allayed when one sees how clumsily and obviously he drives his way through the scene.

The final prose passage, in the fourth group of additions (III, xii A in Boas' text), presents an altogether different problem. The conversation of Iaques and Pedro has prepared the audience for a mad Hieronimo; and, indeed, the latter's wild talk on entering might well convince one of his insanity. But he is quick enough to deny it when the others charge him with it, and the total effect he gives is one of great mental stress, not necessarily mingled with madness.

When the Painter comes, with the improbable tale of his own murdered son, he speaks verse with Hieronimo until the others leave. Hieronimo then changes the form to prose, with an odd introduction:

Come, let's talke wisely now. Was thy Sonne murdered?[16]

It is a little difficult to recapture the peculiar force of the
word "wisely." Hieronimo may mean "seriously," or "to the
point"; the context would support such an interpretation.
But why should a change to prose be necessitated? This
seems to be something more than mad prose. What Hieronimo actually does in this exchange is to give directions to
the Painter in a comparatively formal fashion, although one
realizes perfectly well that he is simply finding a new way
in which to express his grief. He shows good enough sense
in his railing: a quick wit, an almost Hamlet-like pleasure in
the word itself.

> *Painter.* And is this the end?
> *Hier.* O no, there is no end: the end is death and madnesse. As
> I am neuer better then when I am mad: then methinkes I am a braue
> fellow; then I doe wonders: but reason abuseth me, and there's the
> torment, there's the hell. At the last, sir, bringe me to one of the mur-
> derers; were he as strong as *Hector*, thus would I teare and drage him
> vp and downe.[17]

An almost breathless, sobbing note expresses itself in the
rhythms and accents of Hieronimo's speech as well as in the
words themselves:

> *Hier.* Was thy Sonne murdered?
> *Paint.* I, sir.
> *Hier.* So was mine. How doo'st take it? art thou not sometimes mad?
> Is there no trickes that comes before thine eies?[18]

And one hears echoes of Hamlet's conversation with Rosencrantz and Guildenstern in the tone and movement of this
dialogue:

> *Hier.* Canst paint a dolefull crie?
> *Paint.* Seemingly, sir.
> *Hier.* Nay, it should crie; but all is one.[19]

The additions are known to be interpolations by a later
hand. How, then, does this fourth passage, with its prose sequence, fit into the earlier framework? The scene immediately preceding presents a distraught Hieronimo and the King,

who is puzzled but more curious than helpful, in an exchange dominated by Hieronimo's passionate speeches. At this point the additions begin, with the dialogue of Iaques and Pedro. The two are joined by Hieronimo, then by Isabella, and finally by the Painter. Until Hieronimo and the Painter are left alone, the dialogue is in a very moving verse far more subtle and moving than Kyd's. Now the medium shifts to a prose which is no less impressive than this new verse. The function of this prose is to offer a brilliant and strange interlude between Hieronimo's complaints to the King and the wooden Senecan soliloquy which immediately follows. The Painter-episode departs from the mechanical lamentation, whose possibilities have already been exhaustively explored, and portrays Hieronimo's grief in a brilliant, startling and dramatic fashion. The device recalls the use of directions to painters by such later poets as Andrew Marvell, for purposes of both eulogy and satire.

The ending of the scene seems more mystifying than it probably is. Hieronimo "beates the Painter in," after commissioning a painting of himself punishing one of the murderers. This grotesque conclusion resembles the staple matter of Elizabethan comic scenes, but such an interpretation is incredible. It seems more plausible to take this outburst as a final indication that Hieronimo is indeed mad. And, after all, it is madness that explains the action and texture of the entire scene. Hieronimo's preliminary remark, "Come, let's talke wisely now," would have convinced the Elizabethan audience that the poor old man really *was* insane, just as to-day a character in a play or film need only make heated assurances of his sanity to convince everyone that he is actually raving.

The conception and composition of the scene point to a high degree of sophistication in the author of the additions, a sophistication which Ben Jonson, the putative author,

richly possessed. Kyd, as the rest of the play and particularly the other prose scenes bear witness, had no such subtlety of psychology or dramaturgic technique; moreover, at
the time he composed *The Spanish Tragedie*, the use of dramatic prose was, in the main, extremely unsophisticated.
Between Kyd's prose scenes and the prose of the additions
exists a gap comparable to that between Marlowe's comic
scenes and *As You Like It*. And the prose of the additions
looks forward to the prose of *Hamlet*, which represents at its
finest the use of prose for satire and reduction.

It has by now become clear that no single precise and
consistent principle informing the use of prose existed in the
English drama preceding Shakespeare. In the plays here
used as touchstones, in any case, no single principle can be
found. Lyly uses prose largely because it offers him a more
appropriate medium than verse for the exercise of his
peculiar stylistic gifts. Marlowe, Kyd and Greene have
their comic scenes, and Marlowe and Greene their mad
scenes—not to forget the anonymous author of the additions to *The Spanish Tragedie*.

The other playwrights of this period show no startling
divergences from the general pattern. Peele is of some interest because his *Edward I* offers a comparatively early instance of the use of prose for light aristocratic conversation,
possibly indebted to the example of Lyly. Peele's prose is
undeveloped, except in *The Old Wives' Tale* (1595), where
it often shows a startling and realistic vigor. There is also
in this play an episode which bespeaks a certain self-consciousness of technique. Huanebango, in courting Zantippa,
attacks her with Gabriel Harvey's hexameters:

> *Huanebango.* O, that I might, —but I may not, woe to
> my destiny therefore!
> Kiss that I clasp! but I cannot: tell me,
> my destiny, wherefore?

Zantippa (aside). Whoop! now I have my dream. Did you never hear so great a wonder as this, three blue beans in a blue bladder, rattle, bladder, rattle?

Huan. (aside). I'll now set my countenance, and to her in prose; it may be, this rim-ram-ruff is too rude an encounter.[20]

Peele must obviously have thought his audience capable of perceiving and appreciating the difference between prose and verse.

In the earlier Elizabethan drama, then, prose is regularly used for comic scenes and mad scenes. The psychological justification for the use of prose to express madness has already been discussed. The consistency with which prose appears in mad scenes justifies our speaking of this use of prose as conventional; the same may, with certain reservations, be said of the use of prose for comic scenes. Clown-scenes are invariably in prose, but comic scenes in verse also appear, e. g., in *The Knight of the Burning Pestle*. Two other very common conventional uses of prose are in letters and formal documents or proclamations. The formal differentiation of a letter from the play into which it intrudes has been well characterized by Richard David: "The simple contrast, that is the plain verse-prose opposition without any over-tones of character, is . . . common; the most straightforward examples being the letters and proclamations—read matter—which appear as patches of prose in the verse representing the spoken word."[21]

To recapture the effect of such a "patch" of prose, one must remember how different was the Elizabethan drama's use of language from that of the modern drama. The world of the Elizabethan play was created in a language which was patently never spoken in Elizabethan England, a language of greater subtlety and strength than one might expect to find at so comparatively early a stage in the development of the English drama. Verse, as David says, is the staple of the

Elizabethan drama and the idiom of that drama's world. Thus, when the "real world" intrudes, it is formally set off. Comic scenes are marked off in prose: a comic plot may actually be completely dissociated, dramatically and formally, from the main plot of a play. Letters, proclamations, formal discourse of various kinds, are likewise distinct from the poetic world, and their prose is a sign of their being set apart. In our own drama, whose staple is a prose not substantially different from the language we speak, a comparable opposition would require analogous but different techniques, such as the use of business or journalistic jargon.

Prose, then, made its way into the pre-Shakespearean drama for certain conventional purposes; it was used in comic scenes and mad scenes, and for letters and proclamations. To these four prime uses of prose, J. F. Macdonald has added two secondary ones: "The regular speech of the clowns, rustics, and lower characters in general, especially in comedy; the regular speech in ordinary commercial business".[22] Macdonald thus draws a distinction between clown speech and what he calls "comic dialogue, and especially comic scenes from low life," his fourth category. He probably does so because of the necessity for including both Lyly and Marlowe. But can both these uses be termed "conventions"? Except in Lyly's plays, there are few examples before Shakespeare of comic dialogue *not* spoken by clowns. A tendency must become fairly marked before it can properly be called a convention.

Various writers, such as Henry Sharpe and V. F. Janssen, have hopelessly attempted to reduce all the uses of prose to discrete conventions. As long as we know of no Elizabethan style book with precise definitions of the conventions, it would be necessary to reformulate them for each dramatist. Such a task is clearly impossible in the case of Shakespeare, in whose work a principle appears, but who resolves each problem in terms of its own requirements.

It is difficult to ask an unprejudiced observer to accept the hypothesis of the conception, development, and wide acceptance of these dramatic conventions as long as the historical evidence is so incomplete. It is not incredible, however, that this development should have taken place in so comparatively short a time, given the fact that virtually the entire prodigious bulk of the Elizabethan drama was written in London. No playwright was long ignorant of his colleagues' innovations; none can be said to have remained unaffected and uninfluenced by the work of the others. It has become an outworn cliché to compare the Elizabethan drama to the motion picture of our own time, but the comparison may perhaps be invoked once more to serve a double purpose. A device which has once gained popularity in a single film is promptly copied and inserted in a dozen others, however insignificant it may be and however irrelevant dramatically to its new contexts. Similarly, conventional (or, if you will, symbolic) representations in the film have rapidly gained currency, to the point where an attempt to convey a given meaning without using the accepted sign may fail. A familiar example is the cinematic portrayal of madness, which normally requires an actor to assume a fixed stare, to the eerie sound of distant music and the tinkling of small bells. A Hollywood schizoid would today be unrecognizable without these accoutrements. The men who form our taste in such matters apparently feel that the stare and bells are as essential to our awareness of insanity as prose was to the Elizabethan conception. Who can say that prose is the less naturalistic symbol of the two?

III

Dramatic Prose in Later Elizabethan and Jacobean Drama

Shakespeare's prose appears in all its richness and variety when his plays are compared with those of his immediate contemporaries, all of whom made use of prose to some extent. The quality of their prose is often very high; one need only recall the comic prose of Dekker or the strange, melancholy prose of Webster's Flamineo. The line of division between prose and verse is in general clearly marked, although the breakdown of blank verse in the Jacobean drama begins to blur the formal distinction.

What one too rarely finds in these playwrights are the subtle and varied uses of prose, the skillful invention in dramatic technique and style which give Shakespeare's prose its peculiar excellence. Jonson elaborately develops the prose styles of his characters, but he does so in an all-prose play, foregoing the dramatic and stylistic balance which Shakespeare achieves by opposing the two media. Webster keeps the form of the prose-verse play, but reserves prose in the main for a single figure, whose prose then becomes a significant facet of his character. One seeks in vain another Hamlet or Lear or Rosalind, who can speak both prose and verse with consummate skill and beauty. The answer is not far to seek: the creator of Hamlet knew best how Hamlet should speak; another artist capable of creating a Hamlet would not have found problems of technique insuperable.

A brief examination of the uses of prose in the works of Shakespeare's contemporaries and successors, like the study in the previous chapter, will help to establish a basis for judging Shakespeare's achievement and may illuminate some aspects of Shakespeare's practice.

These playwrights often differ in their treatment of common problems of technique; such points of divergence, both significant and insignificant, are interesting as revelatory of the writers' several reactions to a convention of their art, and as such they are of value for this discussion. One cannot use them in the vain hope of establishing the precise influence of Shakespeare's use of prose on his colleagues or of theirs on him, more than to show, as Henry W. Wells has done, that Shakespeare's extensive use of prose established dramatic prose as an important form for other dramatists.[23] It seems, on the whole, less misleading to overemphasize the dramatists' independence than to exaggerate their interdependence.

1. *Jonson*

One can discern in Jonson's plays no single universal principle governing the use of prose and verse. Jonson appears to have made his decision separately for each play; where he found the mixed form suitable, he employed it, as in the humour-plays and in *Poetaster;* where a single medium seemed preferable, he used prose for *Epicœne* and verse for *The Alchemist.* He may have thought that the mixed form diminished the unity of effect; it is hard to believe that any less serious motive could have caused him to eschew prose almost altogether in *The Alchemist.*

Chapman also, in such plays as *The Blind Beggar of Alexandria* (1598), tried his hand at the prose play, but to no great purpose. His work in the mixed form (as in *All Fools* [1605] and *The Gentleman Usher* [1606]) shows no technical originality; his invention appears most effectively in the charming set speech in prose on the Horned Age which concludes *All Fools*. But it is an example of brilliant oratorical prose, not dramatic prose.

What appears to underlie Jonson's willingness to restrict himself to prose or verse is a certain self-consciousness about his craft. In reading his plays, one is often aware of the methodical critic and workman contriving his effects, whereas one rarely catches sight of Shakespeare, who can hardly be imagined planning a play, scene by scene, in terms of a preconceived verse-prose equilibrium. Shakespeare never seems to have thought of writing a play entirely in prose; he may have realized, when he began to write *The Merry Wives of Windsor*, that the greater part of the play would require prose, but it is inconceivable that he calculated nicely the proportions of prose and verse before beginning work. Shakespeare the academic student of dramaturgy does not reveal himself in his plays. But Jonson's plays, even without the evidence of his critical writings, are those of a playwright profoundly and self-consciously preoccupied with the technique of his art.

The fact that Jonson wrote two plays entirely in prose, the elegant *Epicœne* (1609) and the realistic *Bartholomew Fair* (1614), should not be taken to mean that his plays in the mixed form were exceptions to his practice. Actually, he introduced prose passages into two plays otherwise in verse. In *Sejanus* (1603), for example, the first four acts are without prose; in V, x, Jonson presents a meeting of the Senate during which Tiberius's letter proclaims the fall of Sejanus. The opening of the meeting and the letter itself are both in prose. The explanations are simple enough: the Præcon's prose is one of form or ritual, and the prose of the letter goes back to one of the most familiar and earliest conventional usages. The circumstances under which the letter is read contribute to the vigor and movement of the scene. Here is Sejanus, surrounded by sycophants who deluge him with fulsome compliments in verse; suddenly, the voice of the absent Tiberius speaks through his letter in a prose which moves from deliberate obscurity to a dreadful clarity. Arruntius, the gadfly, points out the effect of every phrase on the wavering Senators, their growing indecision and eventual defection. The entire final scene of *Sejanus* is dominated by off-stage action and powers. The letter is an intrusion from without, yet it expresses a power which not even Sejanus can challenge.

The second example of a single prose scene in a verse play is in *Volpone* (1606), II, i. Volpone appears, disguised as a mountebank (for the part of prose in helping to create a disguise cf. *Henry V* or Kent and Edgar in *King Lear*) and touts his snake-oil. His speech is in a known and recognized form, as Peregrine's remarks indicate; the crowd must pay for both the marvelous elixir and the entertainment. Volpone's sales-talk is more than medicine-show jargon; the quality of his hyperbole recalls Marlowe rather than Jeff Peters:

> Here is a poulder, conceal'd in this paper, of which, if I should speake to the worth, nine thousand volumes were but as one page, that page as a line, that line as a word: so short is this pilgrimage of man (which some call life) to the expressing of it. Would I reflect on the price? why, the whole world is but as an empire, that empire as a prouince, that prouince as a banke, that banke as a priuate purse to the purchase of it.[24]

This set speech, intended to render plausible the device by which Volpone communicates with Celia, mimics spiels which Jonson's audience must have known as well as we know them to-day. It belongs to a literary genre that cannot be versified. Jonson wants a street-scene (which his instinct compels him to portray realistically) in which to display the histrionic gifts of his hero, and brings a prose scene into a verse play—a play which many of his colleagues would have been tempted to write largely in prose.

The Alchemist (1610) has two scenes in which prose figures for reasons of convention and dramatic necessity. These scenes, IV, i and ii, present Surly in his Spanish disguise, speaking Spanish prose. One feels certain that Jonson would not have hesitated to try his hand at Spanish verse if he had seen any point in doing so; but Surly is not meant to be understood. He speaks Spanish because he is disguised as a Spaniard, and his lines are not intended to have any other dramatic meaning. The audience understands as much of his speech as is necessary with the help of the stage-business. The Elizabethans were pleased and amused to hear foreign languages on the stage, as *Henry V*, *The Shoemaker's Holiday* and many other plays bear witness; but they were not such sticklers for decorum as to require dramatic verse in those tongues.

Jonson's early mixed plays follow fairly conventional lines. *The Case Is Altered* (published 1609) assigns verse to the serious plot of the nobles, and prose to the low comedians. The witty realist Maximilian speaks prose although he belongs to the noble milieu, and can even cause the aristocrats to follow his example.

Every Man in his Humour (1598) typically makes its effects of contrast by the opposition of consecutive scenes; but Jonson occasionally uses prose and verse within the same scene to produce effects which Shakespeare more commonly achieves by contrasting two scenes. Knowell's verse soliloquy following his introductory verse dialogue with Brainworm is interrupted by Stephen's prose. Knowell then censures Stephen in verse, breaks off while Stephen and a servant converse in prose, and continues with a second denunciation in verse. After a brief prose exchange with the servant, he discusses in verse the ethics of opening the letter addressed to his son, opens and reads it (the letter being, of course, in prose), and then comments savagely on it in verse.

He has a short talk with Brainworm in a kind of formless prose and concludes the scene with another verse soliloquy. The effect of the scene is to make verse the medium of moral indignation and didacticism, while prose, where it is not merely neutral, represents the speech of fops and would-be gallants. Young Knowell's prose letter is effectively framed in a setting of verse speeches and, together with Stephen's silly remarks, forms a gull's horn-book for Old Knowell to attack.

The only prose of the play that has any intrinsic interest is Bobadill's, whether it be his absurd praise of *The Spanish Tragedie* or his advice to earnest young fops. The pleasure one takes in his invention is not so great as that which one feels in watching the free play of Falstaff's versatile wit; without fully accepting Brinsley Nicholson's damaging criticism of Bobadill—"He lies without zest, and invents from mere phlegm"[25]—one may nevertheless admit that there is no great variety in his wit and that it remains always confined within the limits of his humour.

A more specifically satirical play, *Every Man Out of his Humour* (1599), makes much more extensive use of prose. Where *Every Man in his Humour* employs verse quite freely for its more serious characters and action, *Every Man Out of his Humour* limits verse drastically to a few specific functions. The chief verse speaker is Macilente, who, as Asper in the Prologue, first states the theory of humours and principle of the play; he then figures as a character in the play. He is not a "pure" character, in the sense of being conceived in wholly dramatic terms, for he serves as Jonson's spokesman, introducing and defining the humorous characters as precisely as possible. The fact that most of his speeches are monologues is sufficient to explain their being in verse; as late as Wycherley, the speaker of a monologue or soliloquy almost automatically uses verse. Macilente's speeches are not merely comments on action and character; he is the incarnation of envy, and thus speaks not as the dispassionate critic, but as the symbol of the humour of envy. He may obtain satisfaction from the behavior of those whom he observes, or they may drive him to new transports of envy, as when he confesses his desire for Fallace. But he remains true to his humour until purged of it.

The *objective* commentators, Mitis and Cordatus, append their criticisms and discussions to almost every scene. Their remarks, unlike Macilente's, are in prose, for they represent a genuine intrusion from without. They have no part in the action, or, for that matter, in the play at all, whose progress they delay insufferably. Their dialogues tend to follow a single tedious pattern: Cordatus, the informed expositor of the author's intention, answers the naïve questions, objections, and misinterpretations of Mitis. Mitis is nothing more than the author's control; at one point he is specifically identified with the average spectator:

> *Cordatus.* It's the speciall intent of the author, you should [make objections]; for thereby others (that are present) may as well be satisfied, who happily would obiect the same you doe.[26]

Jonson's evident unwillingness to believe that his audience could unaided arrive at a proper understanding of his play shows itself everywhere.

It is to be expected that the action involving the humorous characters of the play should be in prose, for we are shown ridiculous figures in the act of exposing their own follies. Actually there are scenes, or parts of scenes, which do not follow such a rule. Sordido, for example, begins his self-revelation in prose, but concludes it in verse, as the emphasis shifts from his niggardliness to a kind of exaltation of greed. He is no longer merely a man with a humour, but the very incarnation of his vice. In III, ii, he again passes from prose to verse, to mark his conversion. Moreover, the first scene of the over-amorous Deliro and the contemptuous Fallace (II, ii) is in verse perhaps simply because it is a love-scene, although burlesqued. These instances are exceptional; in general, the humours are revealed in prose, to which Macilente's acid verse is the counterpoint.

Verse dominates *Poetaster* (1601) because, one might suppose, of the play's preposterous number of Roman poets. Their sheer quantity is oppressive; any Romans, one expects, would have served quite as well in the supernumerary parts, but Jonson preferred to give even the least significant character an impressive and evocative name. The poets, with a fine sense of decorum, regularly speak verse. Ovid refuses to give up verse in I, i, both as a mode of speech and as a profession, although his father, Tucca, and the rest regularly speak prose. Propertius, Tibullus, and Ovid introduce verse for a sad interlude in the midst of a light conversation (II, i). In III, i, Jonson's version of Horace's encounter with the bore, Horace at first answers Crispinus civilly enough in prose; only his hopeless asides are in verse. At last he loses his temper, drops all pretense of politeness, and openly insults his tormentor in verse.

In these examples, the selection of prose or verse appears to depend upon character, although it also contributes strikingly to dramatic effect, as in the opposition of the two Ovids. In IV, iii, however, a purely dramatic motive underlies the use of prose and verse: Julia and Ovid have a mildly comic scene in prose, which is interrupted by the furious entrance and verse speech of Cæsar. The two parts of the scene are thrown into contrast both with respect to their tone and to the characters of their dominating figures.

During Horace's trial, there is a clear division of prose and verse, verse being reserved for the poets and prose for the comic characters. In the episode of Crispinus' purge, all the characters speak prose because they all participate in the comedy of the poetaster's confusion. The moralizing speeches of Augustus and Virgil bring back verse for a solemn finale, but they are preceded by the no less solemn prose verdict read by Tibullus, and the oath administered to Tucca and Crispinus. The pompous legal prose restores order after the conflict and the comic resolution. The way is prepared for the verse discourses which express the moral of the play.

No great ingenuity is shown in the handling of media in *Poetaster* or in the whole construction of the play: the indecisive and misleading opening, the undramatic introduction of the translations from Horace (except for the bore-scene, which owes its dramatic effectiveness to the Latin original), the implausible and almost ridiculous balcony-scene of Ovid and Julia. The technical handling of verse and prose within the individual scene is always workmanlike and often very good. It is impossible to generalize about its total force in a play whose structure is so uncertain and inconclusive. It is not a coincidence that the best scenes, i.e., the satirical matter, are largely in prose; they constitute Jonson's largest original contribution to the play and draw more heavily on his comic resources than on his classical scholarship.

Cynthia's Revels (1600) may in general be said to follow *Every Man Out of his Humour* in its use of prose and verse. Crites, however, unlike Macilente, enters more freely into the action of the piece because he is associated with Cynthia and the gods, for whom he acts in encompassing the confusion of the humorous characters. The masque-like quality of much of the play permits Jonson to take greater liberties in handling the characters and their interrelations than in a realistic play. One is therefore not conscious of any ambiguity in the character of Crites such as one feels in Macilente. Unlike Macilente, Crites is subject to no restraints; he performs his work of deception, but what he does seems to have little significance or seriousness. People are put out of their humours, as in the earlier "comicall satyres," but where once we saw Carlo Buffone's mouth stuffed with wax, we are now put off with a palinode. *Tout finit par des chansons*. For Crites lacks an inner conflict: he is "a creature of a most perfect and diuine temper. One in whom the humours and elements are peaceably met, without emulation of precedencie";[27] he moves easily from prose to verse, mingling with his gulls (but there is no Sordido here!) and pronouncing Jonson's most deeply moving judgments on human folly.

After the great plays, Jonson turned almost entirely to verse as a dramatic medium. But prose continues to be used in *The New Inn* (1629), *The Staple of News* (1625), and *The Magnetic Lady* (1632). *The New Inn* requires prose only for the rules and regulations of its Court of Love; but the two latter plays employ it for their several equivalents of Cordatus and Mitis, straw figures to drive home Jonson's points in inductions and entr'actes. For prose remained always, to Jonson, the language of criticism.

Jonson's chief contribution to the history of the prose-verse play in English was the creation of a prose comedy which was eventually to supplant the mixed form. His two great prose plays, *Epicœne* and *Bartholomew Fair*, marked the beginning of a tradition of comic dramatic prose that was to reach its height in Restoration comedy. His highly individualistic talent seems to have become ever more dissatisfied with the prose-verse play, perhaps, as has been suggested, because he found it incapable of achieving the unity of tone and effect he sought. Where he dealt in conflicts and oppositions, in the gulling and unmasking of fools, he used the mixed form. But the weird parade of knaves and gulls who ornament Jonson's greatest work offered him no such simple problem, and to solve it he was obliged at the same time to return to earlier forms and to create new ones.

2. *Beaumont and Fletcher*

The old problem of distinguishing the individual contributions of Beaumont and of Fletcher to the works which
bear their names is related to the use the dramatists made
of prose. The traditional method which has been employed
in analyzing their works for the probable share of each author
has been a process of elimination: it can be stated with cer-
tainty that Fletcher alone wrote a given number of the plays;
and the characteristics of his work, subtracted from the
plays written in collaboration with Beaumont, should give
at least some hints about the latter's particular genius. This
is an overstatement of the case: the most that can be asserted
with safety is that Beaumont's collaboration gave a color and
direction to the joint work which one does not find in Fletcher's plays. The technique of collaboration is subject to no
infallible chemical analysis.

For our purposes, the following generalization may be
permitted: the plays in which the two playwrights par-
ticipated have varying quantities of prose; the plays
written by Fletcher alone have almost no prose. (A typical
concession by Fletcher is the prose proclamation of the
Roman general in *Bonduca* [1614], II, ii—a mere observance of convention). Fletcher was able to treat virtually any
subject in his steady, monotonous verse, from the heroics of
Bonduca to the amorous hide-and-seek of *The Wild Goose-
Chase* (1621). No subject, to Fletcher, was too low for verse;
or, rather, no character was admitted who was unable to express himself in the Fletcherian line. Whether Fletcher esche-
wed prose because he felt he had no talent for it, or because
he, like Jonson, found that the mixed form impaired dramatic
unity, cannot be known. At all events, he clearly used prose
only where it seemed absolutely impossible to avoid it.

The Maid's Tragedy (1611) has little prose, almost all of
which is spoken by the bitter Calianax. It seems extraordi-

nary, at first thought, that there should be a place for prose in a tragedy dominated by violence. It should be noted, for example, that the scene in which Evadne's ladies prepare her for her wedding-night substitutes doggerel verse for prose in the ladies' bawdy small talk. The key to Calianax' use of prose seems to be his virtual distraction. He jokes sardonically with Diagoras before the King's masque, and Diagoras can say after him, "He's so humorous since his daughter was forsaken!"[28] Calianax' prose is certainly very close to madness. His grief and frustration drive him to a kind of mad humor in which helplessness and disillusion play equal parts. He cannot find even such expression for his frustration as Aspatia's dirge or Amintor's rage. The old man is unable to do more than perform a "service for him that hath forsaken her." His half-mad prose has a noble simplicity, combined with ironic realism:

My daughter dead here too! And you have all fine new tricks to grieve; but I ne'er knew any but direct crying.[29]

And one must feel in his last words a dignity which does not appear in the unrestrained lyric sobbing of Melantius:

I know not what the matter is, but I am grown very kind, and am friends with you all now. You have given me that among you will kill me quickly; but I'll go home, and live as long as I can.[30]

The prose exposition-scene, familiar from Shakespeare's plays, opens *Philaster* (1611); it is not the only reminiscence of Shakespeare in that wild farrago of scraps from *Hamlet* and *Othello*. The three lords, Dion, Cleremont, and Thrasiline, who set the stage in the first scene, are drawn into the action of the play and thereafter speak prose or verse depending upon the parts they are called upon to play. These three characters normally speak prose when they are commenting on the action or giving exposition, more or less directly, and verse when they actually further the development of the plot. There are, however, exceptions: when Dion is sent by the

King to find out whether Megra is asleep at home (II, iv), he makes his report in prose (although the surrounding dialogue is in verse) because of its semi-comic nature:

Sir, I have asked, and her women swear she is within; but they, I think, are bawds. I told 'em, I must speak with her; they laughed, and said, their lady lay speechless. I said, my business was important; they said, their lady was about it. I grew hot, and cried, my business was a matter that concerns life and death; they answered, so was sleeping, at which their lady was. I urged again, she had scarce time to be so since last I saw her: they smiled again, and seemed to instruct me that sleeping was nothing but lying down and winking. Answers more direct I could not get: in short, sir, I think she is not there.[31]

Whenever, in *Philaster*, promiscuity or illicit sexual relations are treated in comic or semi-comic fashion, prose is regularly used. The characters of the play take an almost inordinate pleasure in gossip, and the Woodmen of IV, ii, appear to be introduced solely for the purpose of further defaming Megra. Why the playwrights continue to rehearse this theme so relentlessly after Megra has satisfactorily exposed herself is a question for the psychoanalyst or the historian of popular taste.

There is no middle ground in *Philaster* between absolute chastity and wanton licentiousness. The impatient Pharamond begs the implacable Arethusa for a foretaste of love in sufficiently crude terms, but does so in verse, for he is at least superficially a lover and suitor. At her refusal and departure, he drops into prose for an almost incredibly candid avowal: "The constitution of my body will never hold out till the wedding; I must seek elsewhere."[32] He pursues the theme in the following act, announcing in prose (II, ii) his intention of attempting the Queen's ladies. His formal verse greeting to Galatea at once warns her of his intentions, and she turns the talk to a light prose dialogue at the close of which she escapes. He then courts Megra in a flowery and conceited verse to which she replies in like terms. Verse is the language of courtship, but Pharamond and Megra reveal interestingly their remarkable self-consciousness about the rules of the game:

> *Megra.* You have in such neat poetry gathered a kiss
> That if I had but five lines of that number
> Such pretty begging blanks, I should commend
> Your forehead or your cheeks, and kiss you too.
> *Pharamond.* Do it in prose; you cannot miss it, madam.[33]

Pharamond thereupon begins the second and more direct stage of his wooing, mocking Arethusa for her frigidity and begging Megra in prose for an assignation. Megra maintains a semblance of virtue by continuing to speak verse, even in the act of granting the rendezvous.

Philaster has one odd departure from the conventions of the earlier Elizabethan drama. The Captain and Citizens, who appear in V, iv, to force the King to restore the throne to Philaster, speak verse, perhaps because they are not rabble but the just instruments of God. In contrast to them, the King, seeing himself and his kingdom imperiled by the mob, loses control of himself and rages in conventional mad prose. He rises to verse once more to appeal to Philaster: but he has meanwhile undergone a change of heart and is no longer a tyrant.

The quasi-comic scenes involving De Vitry, a disbanded officer, account for most of the prose in *Thierry and Theodoret* (published 1621). De Vitry is made to appear a kind of plain dealer; he accepts money for helping to build up the myth of Protaldy's valiance (III, ii), but his honor will not suffer the affront of a blow. He concludes his arrangement with Bawdber in prose, but changes immediately afterwards to verse to express his shame:

> After that rate, I and my friends would beggar the kingdom.
> Sir, you have made me blush to see my want,
> Whose cure is such a cheap and easy purchase:
> This is male-bawdry, belike.[34]

Thus his conflicting feelings bring about a change of form within a single speech.

In the final act, De Vitry jests with the soldiers in prose, and, in the same medium, carries through the intrigue against Protaldy. But directly he discovers Protaldy's villainy, his new mission as the avenger of Theodoret makes him change to verse, while the soldiers naturally continue in prose.

Much the same pattern appears in *A King and No King* (1611), where prose is spoken by Mardonius, the blunt and honest soldier; Bessus, the braggart captain, who is the center of most of the play's humor; and the group of citizens whose bawdy and homely conversation provides a realistic frame for the scene of Arbaces' victorious return from the wars (II, ii).

Beaumont and Fletcher's most interesting experiment with prose is in their masterpiece, *The Knight of the Burning Pestle* (1609). The alternation between prose and verse is somewhat complicated by the quantity of prose in the play. The ways in which it is used fall largely into three categories: the interruptions of the Citizen and his wife; the comic scenes involving the Merrythoughts; and scenes involving Ralph, the Knight of the Burning Pestle. Verse is reserved for the romantic plot, and, naturally, for Ralph's heroics.

The Knight of the Burning Pestle is for many reasons unique in the Beaumont and Fletcher canon. It is the one play in which the collaborators permitted prose to be the basic form and parodied their own verse and that of other playwrights. It may even be maintained that there is only burlesque verse in the play. Humphrey can declare his love in such verse and in no other:

> Fair Mistress Luce, how do you? are you well?
> Give me your hand, and then I pray you tell
> How doth your little sister and your brother;
> And whether you love me or any other...

> Let no game
> Or any other thing that tendeth to the same,
> Be ever more remembered, thou fair killer,
> For whom I sate me down, and brake my tiller.[35]

Much of the prose in the play proper is also burlesque. Ralph loses no time in adapting the language of Palmerin to his own situation:

> There are no such courteous and fair well-spoken knights in this age: they will call one "the son of a whore" that Palmerin of England would have called "fair sir;" and one that Rosicleer would have called "right beauteous damsel," they will call "damned bitch." . . .
>
> Why should not I, then, pursue this course, both for the credit of myself and our company? for amongst all the worthy books of achievements I do not call to mind that I yet read of a grocer errant: I will be the said knight.—Have you heard of any that hath wandered unfurnished of his squire and dwarf? My elder prentice Tim shall be my trusty squire, and little George my dwarf. Hence, my blue apron! Yet in remembrance of my former trade, upon my shield shall by portrayed a Burning Pestle, and I will be called the Knight of the Burning Pestle. . . .
>
> My beloved squire, and George my dwarf, I charge you that from henceforth you never call me by any other name but "the right courteous and valiant Knight of the Burning Pestle;" and that you never call any female by the name of woman or wench, but "fair lady," if she have her desires, if not, "distressed damsel;" that you call all forests and heaths "deserts," and all horses "palfreys."[36]

Prose has yet a more basic function. It is the bedrock of the play. The Citizen and his wife, the omnipresent and implacable arbiters of the scene, who force Ralph into a play where he has no place, speak a common, not to say a vulgar prose; their dialogue reproduces, with a fidelity that recalls Dekker, the authentic accents of the London lower classes. The Citizen guards jealously the honor of his trade and misses no opportunity to exalt it. His interruptions of the play are provoked by his pride, both professional and civic, in contrast to his wife's scatterbrained comments on the action and injunctions to Ralph. And every word they speak reinforces the ridiculousness of the play and its action. Ralph's scenes are, after all, no more preposterous than the romantic plot of the play; and the speech of Ralph as May-Lord is far superior to any of the play's "serious" verse.

In the prose of *The Knight of the Burning Pestle* is the play's great energy. The two highly critical London bourgeois will not suffer boredom after the genteel example of their betters, but break in unabashed when the action drags or the inspiration is insufficient. They are calmly certain that Ralph's part cannot be dull; they suggest the whole conception of the character and the types of scenes in which he shall be made to appear, and he is never disappointing. The Citizen and his wife reveal a fact to which almost the whole of Elizabethan drama testifies: simple and boisterous prose comedy, from Launce to Falstaff, was a sovereign aid to any play. If the comic material did not precisely or even approximately complement the serious action, so much the worse for the serious action. It was left, as in this play, to its own devices, and could be shooed off the stage if it too long delayed the return of the clowns.

In fine, one cannot say that Beaumont and Fletcher made any substantial contribution to the development of dramatic prose. They put their finest prose into *The Knight of the Burning Pestle,* but it is the only play in which humble characters have more than walk-on parts. Beaumont and Fletcher's characters were ordinarily created to speak exactly such verse as is assigned to them, a verse which almost automatically excludes the possibility of their speaking any prose at all—of which the logical result is seen in the later verse plays of Fletcher. (Fletcher's characteristic line, with its extra syllable, has a decidedly colloquial rhythm and may therefore have been conveniently employed in many situations where another dramatist might have used prose.)

An opposition between verse and prose is infrequently used for characterization, as in the figure of Calianax; the playwrights seem not to have been greatly interested in such experiments, however, but depended for characterization upon their usual alternation of drawing and sheathing swords. The type of play which had made Beaumont and Fletcher enormously popular allowed little scope for prose. *The Knight of the Burning Pestle* was, be it remembered, a failure in the theatre—and Beaumont and Fletcher presumably had the professional writer's natural reluctance to produce failures.

3. *Dekker*

Dekker is one of the most engaging prose writers of the Elizabethan era. His non-dramatic writings rather than his plays have doubtless won him his renown; but one is hardly surprised to find in the plays the same force and zest which make the *Guls Horn-Booke* and the pamphlets such brilliant performances.

Dekker establishes in his plays a rough division of prose for comic and verse for serious parts, and regularly uses prose for realistic effects. His comic passages are in prose because they are realistic as well as comic. Such is the basis for the distribution in *The Shoemaker's Holiday* (1600). The story of Simon Eyre and his friends and fellows is told in the rough-and-tumble Rabelaisian prose it deserves and requires; the romantic plot is in verse and quite obviously had only secondary interest for its author. He could hardly have brought himself otherwise to allow Sybil's unbroken flow of lewd and slangy abuse to interrupt Rose's romantic monologue (II, i). The play which depicts the rise to glory of a humble shoemaker is written in the belief that no serious action exists which cannot be reduced to laughter.

Prose, formerly the caste-mark of the common man, now becomes the symbol of his plain and honest worth. Hammon

4

conducts his suit of Jane in verse and at the last attempts to persuade Ralph to give her up for £20:

> *Hammon.* Say, wilt thou freely cease thy claim in her,
>   And let her be my wife?
> *All.*   No, do not, Ralph.
> *Ralph.* Sirrah Hammon, Hammon, dost thou think a shoemaker is so base to be a bawd to his own wife for commodity? Take thy gold, choke with it! Were I not lame, I would make thee eat thy words![37]

The moral superiority of the commoner to the gentleman is also the theme of *The Honest Whore* (1604), in which the division of media is affected by moral rather than social considerations. Matheo, the wastrel and seducer, speaks only prose under all circumstances. Bellafront has prose in the long first part of II, i, where she appears as an unreformed prostitute; but the conversion which Hippolito's denunciation effects causes Bellafront henceforth to speak only verse, the external symbol of her reformation. This change becomes still more striking when it is contrasted with the unregenerate prose of Matheo and his friends in III, iii.

The final scene of the play, in the madhouse of Bedlam, shows an interesting and somewhat intricate interweaving of prose and verse. The Friar, Hippolito, Matheo, and Infelice enter, discussing the secret marriage which the Friar is to perform. Matheo alone speaks prose. The Duke and his attendants engage in a short verse conversation and then question in prose a sweeper in the madhouse. This dialogue is grotesquely humorous. An exhibition of madmen follows, leading to the entrance of Bellafront. The appearance of each madman is preceded by Anselmo's description (in verse) of his case; the conversation between each madman and his visitors, however, is in prose. These exchanges are little more than long raving speeches by the madmen and a few short answers from the onlookers. Bellafront begins in prose, then, in reading the palms of the pretended friars, gives her judgments in a verse whose short irregular line resembles the verse which Shakespeare uses for charms, incantations, and prophecies. She returns to prose after the Duke has discovered and forgiven Infelice and Hippolito, and artfully introduces her revelations about Matheo into her babbling. When Matheo is trapped, Bellafront promptly reveals herself as sane—and returns to verse. As she no longer needs to counterfeit insanity, she is free to cast off the disguise of prose.

The subordinate plots of the draper Candido and his wife are virtually parallel in the two parts of the play. Candido almost always speaks verse, as a sign of his equanimity and nobility of character, while his tormentors (who are little more than clowns of the lowest order) speak prose. He reads the Duke a lesson in verse on the necessity of patience at the end of Part I. Verse is his particular privilege because he is less a true character than a virtue out of a morality play.

The Second Part of *The Honest Whore* (published 1630) introduces two new prose characters: Bryan, the Irish clown, and Orlando Friscobaldo. Bryan speaks comic prose which needs no explanation. Friscobaldo speaks prose in his character as an honest, downright man, the only kind of *deus ex machina* that Dekker could have tolerated. He is best fitted, by his own virtuousness, to describe the virtuous man; but Dekker must have felt some compunction about putting so much serious verse into Friscobaldo's mouth, and consequently cast the speech in sententious couplets, presenting the whole as a quotation. To emphasize the point, he allowed Friscobaldo to add a prose exposition, the style of which is decidedly more characteristic of the old man.

A horrendous scene in Bridewell, paralleling the Bedlam-scene of the First Part, ends the Second Part. As before, the individual whores speak chiefly prose monologues, against which stand the verse speeches of the Duke and the Masters of Bridewell. If this final scene is at all disappointing, it may be because Dekker's motives in presenting this parade of horribles seem not entirely clear. At the end of Part I, the masque of madmen came to a climax with the appearance of the supposedly deranged Bellafront. In Part II, on the other hand, Bellafront has been vindicated and the dénouement is complete before Dorothea Target and her colleagues appear. The characters of the four whores are adroitly contrasted; but it is difficult to believe that the desire to portray such a contrast was Dekker's chief inspiration. Rather is it apparent that Dekker was eager to give his play a shocking and effective climax, and he stuck at no implausibility to do so. The noble spectators of the whores' disgrace are vastly amused by the whole business, and the audience in the theatre doubtless shared their pleasure.

Friscobaldo's tirades are the best prose in *The Honest Whore*. Dekker has created a character in prose whom Shakespeare might well have envied him. Friscobaldo and Simon Eyre are Dekker's great contributions to the small gallery of great prose characters in the Elizabethan drama, figures whose personalities are conceived entirely in prose, and who do not normally speak verse in their own person. Their use of prose, above all, conveys their profoundly realistic view of life and their essentially human qualities, interests, and activities. Unlike the great poetic and tragic figures, they live on an altogether human plane; and their prose perfectly reflects their philosophy.

Dekker's plays helped to associate prose with realism, thereby giving Elizabethan dramatic prose its most significant line of development. Shakespeare gave the greatest impetus to this tendency by the sheer volume as well as the beauty and variety of his dramatic prose. Dekker's achievement was not so great, but he earned his place in a great dramatic tradition by wedding prose and realism in some of the Elizabethan drama's most brilliant productions.

4. *Middleton*

Middleton's plays, and those written by him in collaboration with Rowley, make use of prose in the simple and uninspired fashion which at times must seem the norm in the Elizabethan drama. The restriction of prose to the comic matter of a play is particularly marked in Middleton and Rowley's works, in which one may see the natural result of a tendency towards an ever stricter division between the comic and serious plots. *A Fair Quarrel* (1617), for example, does not make even a token gesture of relating its two actions. In such plays prose appears only in the subordinate comic plots and in the mouths of the omnipresent comic characters, who wander freely through both plots and who speak prose wherever they go. Almost none of this prose deserves more than passing mention.

The striking exception among these plays is Middleton's *A Trick to Catch the Old One* (1608), whose success in combining prose and verse may be explained in part by its unusually fine dramatic unity. *A Trick to Catch the Old One* in fact introduces no subordinate plot at all, but develops incidents which grow naturally out of the main plot. The play appears to have been conceived largely in prose, and the fact that prose is here permitted to play more than a secondary rôle doubtless explains its very excellence. It is deplorable but wholly natural that a playwright who is accustomed to employ prose for comic scenes and interludes in which he takes little interest should take no great care in handling this inferior medium. But it is likewise to be expected that, in working on a boisterous comedy in which verse will necessarily count for much less than prose, the playwright will endeavor to make of his prose an effective vehicle for his play.

The verse of *A Trick to Catch the Old One* comes chiefly in burlesque passages: Hoard and Lucre rant in verse, the Courtesan plays the demure young widow in verse, Witgood cozens his creditors and apostrophizes his mortgage in verse. The contrast of this verse with the staple prose of the play is extremely comic. The interactions of prose and verse in this play are so cleverly contrived that Middleton's failure to repeat this delightful experiment is regrettable.

5. *Webster*

Webster, who may justly be considered Shakespeare's only peer as a dramatic poet, comes nearest to him also in the intricate beauty of his prose. No other writer for the Elizabethan stage, after Shakespeare, was able to blend prose and verse with the exquisiteness of Webster; Tourneur approached him in the quality and movement of his prose, but left us no such characters as Flamineo and Bosola.

Almost all the prose in each of Webster's two great tragedies is spoken by a single character. In each play, this character is a villain, a strange, humorous, and cynical creature. The evil which the action of both plays portrays finds verbal expression through these two men. Such is their influence over others that no one in either play speaks prose except in their company. Cynicism, gall, and a perverted sententiousness make up their philosophy and their speech.

Flamineo, in *The White Divel* (1612), tells us in an aside:

> I do put on this feigned Garbe of mirth,
> To gull suspition.[38]

But he does not need to explain any single action to us in these terms. His curious mirth is ever with him; he is the clown in a play which could tolerate only so strange a clown. His is a humor that affords no relief from the play's horrors, but, on the contrary, gives them a fuller meaning by moralizing them. Flamineo's prose is a glittering garment in

which he cloaks himself before all men; it both shields him
from the world and presents the world with just such a picture
of himself as he wants conveyed. He is supremely self-conscious, inordinately proud of his wit. Witness his dying words:

> I recover like a spent taper, for a flash
> And instantly go out.

Let all that belong to Great men remember th'ould wi[v]es tradition, to be like the Lyons ith Tower on Candlemas day, to mourne if
the Sunne shine, for feare of the pittiful remainder of winter to come.

> 'Tis well yet there's some goodnesse in my death,
> My life was a blacke charnell: I have c[a]ught
> An everlasting could. I have lost my voice
> Most irrecoverably: Farewell glorious villaines,
> "This busie trade of life appeares most vaine,
> "Since rest breeds rest, where all seeke paine by paine.
> Let no harsh flattering Bels resound my knell,
> Strike thunder, and strike lowde to my farewell.[39]

In this speech, Flamineo uses, respectively, blank verse,
prose, blank verse again, and finally couplets. In another
playwright, this variety might seem to indicate a breakdown
of forms, but not in Webster, who was supremely conscious
of the peculiar powers inherent in each form. The effect
would seem to be the following: Flamineo announces that
he has yet some message to convey—and that prose message
is the crystallization of all his wit and disillusion. He returns
to blank verse, knowing that death is approaching, and can-
didly sums up his life. At the last, he compresses all his
cynical view of life into a sententious couplet, but reserves
his concluding couplet for himself: no funeral bell can toll
the passing of so great a villain; only a thunderclap can serve.
Thus the three forms are all employed together for a final
effect.

Flamineo seems always aware that he courts suspicion by
his strange behavior and speech, and so explains more than

once that he is playing the madman. His explanation of his strange mirth at the house of Monticelso has been noted; after the trial, he says again:

> Because now I cannot counterfeit a whining passion for the death of my Lady, I will faine a madde humor for the disgrace of my sister, and that will keepe off idle questions.—Treasons tongue hath a villainous palsy in't, I will talk to any man, heare no man, and for a time appeare a polliticke mad-man.[40]

Does Webster perhaps feel unable to convince his audience that a character who speaks in Flamineo's accustomed style is believable unless he insists on his feigned madness? Some such self-consciousness is apparently involved, for Flamineo can tell Brachiano and Vittoria his prose parable of the crocodile and the bird, and add in an aside:

> It may appeare to some ridiculous
> Thus to talke knave and madman; and sometimes
> Come in with a dried sentence, stuft with sage.
> But this allowes my varying of shapes,
> *Knaves do grow great by being great mens apes.*[41]

Flamineo's flexible prose, which is rendered at once brilliant and direct by its colloquialism, creates a figure who moves with ease and rapidity in a world peopled by far stronger men. So much does Flamineo dominate the prose in *The White Divel* that he can rewrite the conventions for its use. In IV, i, he reads aloud a letter to Vittoria which Brachiano has intercepted. The convention governing the use of prose for letters is one of the oldest; but now, because it is Flamineo who reads the letter and interpolates remarks concerning it, the letter is put into verse (the superscription, as read by Brachiano, is in the usual prose) so that Flamineo's comments may still be in prose. Webster does not violate decorum; he simply creates a new decorum:

> *Your teares Ile turne to triumphes, bee but mine.*
> *Your prop is fall'n; I pittie that a vine*
> *Which Princes heretofore have long'd to gather,*
> *Wanting supporters, now should fade and wither.*

Wine yfaith, my Lord, with lees would serve his turne.
> *Your sad imprisonment Ile soone uncharme,*
> *And with a princelie uncontrolled arme*
> *Lead you to Florence, where my love and care*
> *Shall hang your wishes in my silver haire.*

A halter on his strange aequivocation!
> *Nor for my yeares returne mee the sad willow —*
> *Who prefer blossomes before fruit that's mellow?*

Rotten on my knowledge with lying too long i'th bed-straw.
> *And all the lines of age this line convinces:*
> *The Gods never wax old, no more doe Princes.*

A pox on't—teare it, let's have no more Atheists
For Gods sake.[42]

Two other exceptions to an equally familiar convention
are less easily explained, especially since Webster conforms
elsewhere in the play. Brachiano on his death-bed, and Cornelia at the winding of Marcello's corpse, are described in
stage-directions as speaking in "several forms of distraction,"
yet they speak verse; however, Cornelia speaks deranged
prose at the scene of Marcello's murder. Webster perhaps intended to give Brachiano some last shadow of dignity in his death, and therefore violated the convention. The
same may be said of the dirge-scene; the lyricism is stronger
than the "distraction," and triumphs over the convention.
Webster is daring enough to flout the convention as Shakespeare never did; but he departs from the forms so rarely
that he cannot have consciously intended to destroy the convention which he elsewhere so successfully exploited.

Webster has no prose-speaker to rival Flamineo; others
merely speak prose from time to time, as the situation may
require, but Flamineo's native speech is prose. His verse is
excellent, but cannot convey to the fullest the mockery and
cynicism which find their finest expression in prose, and
which connect Flamineo with Hamlet; compare his prose,
for example, with the sardonic prose of Hamlet in conversation with Rosencrantz and Guildenstern. The Elizabethan

drama is full of arrant scoundrels who speak verse; but
Webster was too great an artist not to know that this disillusioned paragon of Machiavellianism could expose himself
most fittingly in prose.

The rôle of Bosola in *The Duchess of Malfi* (1614) is the
one most analogous to Flamineo's, but Bosola does not dominate his play's prose to so great a degree because he is at
once less complex and less disillusioned than Flamineo. At
his first appearance, he reveals the bitterness and disillusion
that are characteristic of Flamineo, but on a lower level; he is
the hired bully made startlingly articulate, perhaps by his "foul
melancholy." These two words of Antonio's alone prepare us
for the extraordinary development of Bosola's character.

The same scene presents Ferdinand jesting with his attendants in prose. Antonio then draws the Cardinal's character for Delio:

> Some such flashes superficially hang on him, for forme: but ob-
> serve his inward Character: he is a melancholly Churchman: The
> Spring in his face, is nothing but the Ingendring of Toades: where he
> is jealous of any man, he laies worse plots for them, then ever was im-
> pos'd on *Hercules*: for he strewes in his way Flatterers, Panders, Intel-
> ligencers, Athiests, and a thousand such politicall Monsters: he should
> have beene Pope: but in stead of comming to it by the primative decensie
> of the church, he did bestow bribes, so largely, and so impudently, as
> if he would have carried it away without heavens knowledge...[43]

He goes on to describe Ferdinand in verse. Why this
change? The account of the Cardinal speaks for itself. But
the description of the Duke, twice interrupted by Delio, is
relatively short and unremarkable. In the middle of his last
speech, Antonio breaks off and leaves the brothers to speak
of the Duchess in terms of rare beauty. The anticipation of
this poetic passage may have persuaded Webster to put the
matter immediately preceding it into verse.

Bosola gives promise, in his two dialogues with the old
lady, of developing the theme of his cynical melancholy; but

he speaks very little prose after Act II, performing his duties with a minimum of words, and reassumes his characteristic speech only in the scene of the Duchess' murder (IV, ii). This scene is unquestionably the most celebrated in Webster's work. The Duchess' calm verse is contrasted first with the prose of the lunatics, and then with that of the disguised Bosola. The latter comes to her with sententious sermonizing on the transitoriness of life. The Duchess cuts him short with "I am Duchess of Malfi still," and her dignity shocks Bosola into verse. The Duchess can yet take the initiative: "Let me be a little merry," she says, and begins a semi-humorous prose debate with Bosola, who then reads her another prose sermon. Now she knows her doom and asks to be told plainly. Her speech restores verse even before the entrance of the Executioners forces the scene to yet a higher tragic level.

The humor of Webster's characters is a mad and melancholy one. If he makes such abundant use of prose in his two tragedies, it is because his prose characters are grim clowns. Not that Flamineo or Ferdinand or Bosola or the madmen are in any sense funny; it is instructive to compare the mad scene in *The Duchess of Malfi* with the gay visit to Bedlam in *The Honest Whore*. But surely there are certain analogies of pattern between Webster's "clowns" and the commoner variety.

Webster adapted prose to his own purposes in a masterly way, taking his cue from *Hamlet* and the additions to *The Spanish Tragedie*. Only in Shakespeare's plays is brilliant prose employed so superbly for dramatic effect. Webster had Shakespeare's knack of building up a complete character in prose; he was able both to exploit the prose convention to the fullest and to violate it when necessary. His prose contributes enormously to the creation of the sinister atmosphere which pervades his plays.

6. *Ford*

Ford's technique in the use of prose may almost be taken as a survey of the history of Elizabethan dramatic prose, for it contains all the elements observed in his predecessors and contemporaries. He himself made little or no contribution to the development of dramatic prose, but effectively used the traditions as he found them.

Thus, for example, the prose of *Perkin Warbeck* (1634) is precisely at the stage of development of the Cade scenes in *2 Henry VI*, although Ford's play was written at least forty years after Shakespeare's play. The prose speakers are Warbeck's dubious counsellors, whose low birth and comic rôles account for their prose. One is tempted to think that Ford was doing his best to ape the forms of the old plays; at the same time, it must be remembered that these characters serve a dramatic purpose in that their very presence casts a certain suspicion on Warbeck.

If *Perkin Warbeck* is of little more than antiquarian interest to this study, *The Lover's Melancholy* (1629), *Love's Sacrifice* (1633), and *'Tis Pity She's A Whore* (1633) show Ford to be at least as advanced in the use of prose as Webster. The two latter plays have a common feature: each has a sinister, Machiavellian figure who is chiefly instrumental in arranging the catastrophe, and who moves through the play as a cynical villain who almost alone uses prose. But these characters differ in their villainous techniques and consequently in their prose styles. D'Avolos is an Iago conceived by a dramatist less gifted than Shakespeare; Vasques recalls the villains of Webster, less brilliant in conception and execution because his rôle is simpler and less interesting than that of a Flamineo or Bosola.

Ford has also his positive character, the disillusioned man who has not turned knave, such as Rhetias in *The Lover's Melancholy*. He speaks prose because he is cynical about the court and its ways; he has been reduced from a courtier to a simple man, a plain dealer. He moves among the parasites of the court and mocks them; but he is also a positive worker for good. He is over-blunt; by making him change from prose to verse, Ford is careful to convey Rhetias' feeling that he has exceeded himself in recalling to Palador the circumstances of Eroclea's flight:

> *Rhetias.* Now, noble sir, if you did love the Lady Eroclea, why may not such safety and fate direct her as directed the other? 'tis not impossible.
>   *Palador.* If I *did* love her, Rhetias! Yes, I did.
>   Give me thy hand: as thou didst serve Meleander,
>   And art still true to these, henceforth serve me.
>   *Rhetias.* My duty and my obedience are my surety;
>   But I have been too bold.[44]

The Lover's Melancholy has its share of comic prose, in which it parallels the comic aspects of the sub-plots in *'Tis Pity She's A Whore* and *Love's Sacrifice*. It is striking that Ford made the quasi-comic subplots of the two latter plays conform in matter and treatment to the principal plots of the plays more carefully than in *The Lover's Melancholy*. Ford clearly had the good taste to recognize that the too-familiar Elizabethan divergence between the tragic and comic actions had become unthinkable for the writer who aspired to be more than a hack. Comedy, of a sort, has its place in tragedy; but since it is of necessity the matter of the sub-plot, it must be made to serve the purpose of the play as a whole. The clowns did not always have to "laugh, to set on some quantity of barren spectators to laugh too"; too often, the playwright had taken that task upon himself.

The use of prose for the depiction of cynical, lecherous characters has already been noted in Dekker's plays. Ford does the same with Ferentes, in *Love's Sacrifice*. This usage is bound up with the expression of realism and denigration in prose. Matheo and Ferentes are gallants whose way of life necessarily involves cynicism and cold-bloodedness. The realistic portrayal of such men is most effectively accomplished through the use of prose. Moreover, their bawdy conversation partakes, to varying degrees, of the comic.

Prose probably found no place in Ford's conception of *The Broken Heart* because of the unreality that shrouds his Sparta. His Italy is far more tangible; it is a luxurious land where people are moved by strange and fascinating passions and vices. His Sparta is, by contrast, a land in the sky; dreadful things are done there, but a veil separates them from the audience. *'Tis Pity She's A Whore* has a stark immediacy of effect, and its characters therefore require more drastic differentiation than do the somewhat misty figures of *The Broken Heart*.

Ford is the last great Elizabethan dramatist to work in the mixed form. Between him and the Restoration lies a great gulf, bridged in matter and approach by Shirley, but in form by no playwright. It is wholly comprehensible that the later comedy should have chosen prose as its form (although odd vestiges of the mixed form remain, as in *The Plain Dealer*, and the externals of the form linger on in some of the heroic plays), for it was a comedy of cynical realism. The movement of Shakespeare's contemporaries and successors was toward the greater use of prose for realism; in this respect, none surpassed Shakespeare.

The later Elizabethan drama is disappointing if one expects to find a consistent development of the verse-prose form. The majority of the playwrights observed the conventions and devices which had grown up around the use of prose, but, as a group, did little to advance the form. Individual writers in fact produced intelligent and imaginative plays in which one or another aspect of dramatic prose was carried forward. Jonson revealed the possibilities of an all-prose play, virtually neglected since Lyly; Webster and Ford advanced the art of characterization in prose. A good deal of the work in this form had great literary merit and helped prepare the advent of prose as the dominant and later the sole form for drama. But many writers were content to regard prose as the inferior medium in which to cast comic matter, and their work, from a technical standpoint, shows no advance over the plays of the early Elizabethans.

Prose in the Elizabethan drama began with the plays of Lyly, but only Jonson followed Lyly's lead in attempting all-prose plays, and then with quite different motives. The prose conventions—letters, proclamations, madness, and humor —won ready acceptance, and one can follow them without difficulty into the late Jacobean drama. But that continuity is in itself meaningless. The lowest common denominator of prose consisted in the observance of the four conventions, and nothing more. The elaboration and development of the convention to include such qualities as cynicism, disillusion, realism and the supremely important use of prose for purposes of denigration came more slowly and unevenly. This development appears at its most advanced stage in Shakespeare's work; Webster and others also exploited the convention to the full, but were capable of violating it.

We cannot know with what degree of consciousness the Elizabethan playwright approached the problem of using prose. He probably had, at the beginning, a more or less clear conception of the type of situation that required prose; from that point on, he was guided only by his intelligence and daring. The independence with which the leading play-wrights treated the prose convention makes it difficult to derive a unified course of development from the comparison of all their plays. Jonson, for example, stands apart when considered as a writer of dramatic prose, just as he is unique with respect to many other problems of the Elizabethan drama. Beaumont and Fletcher, who seem not to have been greatly interested in the whole question, pay a minimal obedience to the convention; but on one splendid occasion, in *The Knight of the Burning Pestle*, they produced a play in which all the techniques are brilliantly interwoven. Heywood, whose bourgeois subjects offer him ample opportunity for the use of prose, has but little prose and uses that little poorly. Webster, Tourneur, and Ford employ the convention with great art within a limited frame. Their inspiration apparently comes from Shakespeare, and specifically from the Shakespeare of *Hamlet*. Their prose-speaking characters reduce and denigrate the world in a bitter and cynical prose: "this goodly frame, the earth" becomes "a sterile promontory." The prose convention, in the hands of these last playwrights of the great age, is in large part a technique of reduction.

Such a generalization cannot be made for all the dramatists under discussion, because one must allow both for individual variation of ability and intention, and for certain larger technical trends. A decline in the regularity of blank verse becomes increasingly marked in the later Elizabethans and Jacobeans; and, where the formal and regular qualities of blank verse are no longer very apparent, the distinction between verse and prose is meaningless and, indeed, impossible. Thus Fletcher, for example, toward the end of his career gives up prose almost entirely.

What relation does the work of Shakespeare bear to that of his contemporaries and successors? His extensive and varied use of prose gave impetus and direction to those of his fellows who also saw great technical potentialities in the convention: Dekker and Beaumont and Fletcher found a realism in prose that was denied to verse. *The Shoemaker's Holiday*, *The Honest Whore*, *The Knight of the Burning Pestle* owe their realistic effects to a free and imaginative use of prose. Webster, Tourneur, and Ford, with a quite different dramatic intent, saw in Shakespeare's use of prose for denigration a model to be followed. Webster, surely the most gifted of the three, is closest to Shakespeare and probably the most successful practitioner, after Shakespeare, in this form. But where Webster was capable of violating the convention, Shakespeare extended it. This comparison reaffirms the rich conservatism of Shakespeare, who found a convention, developed it greatly in many directions, but never cast it aside. Webster was a more daring experimenter, who observed the convention as long as it served his dramatic ends. The more diverse uses of prose that he might have found in Shakespeare's comedies appear not to have interested him.

Tourneur followed Shakespeare in the use of prose for reduction, but within the limits of his own ability and taste. Vendice of *The Revenger's Tragedy* (1601) speaks a cynical prose which doubtless owes its inspiration to the example of Hamlet. But the graveyard scene in *The Atheist's Tragedy* (1611), which also is derived from *Hamlet*, is a mockery. A prose speech begun in Hamlet's style soon drops into sententious verse. The nuances and contrasts of the scene Tourneur imitates are completely lost, and sensational effects predominate.

For the most part, one finds few direct connections between Shakespeare's work and that of his contemporaries and successors with respect to the prose convention. Parallels for various stages of his development in the convention exist in the works of his fellows, but in no one man is there so clear-cut a development as in Shakespeare. The total impression given by their work is confused and even chaotic; Shakespeare's achievement gains in magnitude by comparison. He had a broader and more comprehensive view of all the implications of the convention, and an account of this relatively minor aspect of his work is a microcosm of his whole technique.

5

IV

Shakespeare: The Comedies

In prose, comedy finds a medium in which it can easily and naturally express itself. Verse implies tension, pattern, formalism; prose, freedom and relaxation. Verse is the proper vehicle for high passion; prose, for rational discussion and calm resolution. The tragic problem culminates in action; the comic problem, in words.

It is, therefore, altogether just that Shakespeare should have employed prose extensively in his comedies from the outset of his career. Prose occupies one-fourth to one-third of the text of the early comedies, but it grows steadily in bulk and importance until it reaches a somewhat dubious apogee in *The Merry Wives of Windsor*, in which the verse is on all counts virtually insignificant. The late comedies show a decline in the quantity of prose, but the form loses nothing of its special function or value.

Henry W. Wells has argued cogently in his "The Continuity of Shakespearean Prose"[45] for a conception of Shakespeare's prose as a mature, fully realized medium from the earliest plays onwards. The verse style, according to Wells, undergoes constant development throughout Shakespeare's career; but the prose of Launce is already rich and mature. One can hardly deny that Wells is correct in challenging the lay reader to assign a given prose passage from Shakespeare to the early, middle, or late portion of Shakespeare's career; a similar experiment with a passage of verse would be palpably less difficult.

Is not the explanation of this continuity to be found in the debt of Shakespeare's prose to the colloquial speech in which it is rooted? This element of everyday life, expressing itself largely in the realism of comic prose and thus affecting not only the medium but the employment of that medium in the Elizabethan drama, remains a constant from *The Two Gentlemen of Verona* to *The Tempest*. When, with Wells, we praise Shakespeare for his early maturity in the writing of prose, we are in fact saying that he was able from the beginning to make effective use of his observation of life in Elizabethan England. Nor are we dispraising his verse in thus praising his prose; no one is likely to deny that a poet requires full maturity in life and in art for the creation of *King Lear*.

1. *Love's Labour's Lost*

It is a commonplace to say that Shakespeare's use of prose in *Love's Labour's Lost* (1595) was influenced by Lyly's prose comedies; something of this influence has already been discussed. The mark of Euphuism is doubtless on *Love's Labour's Lost*; it is nevertheless worth noting that well over half of Shakespeare's play is in verse. There is a gross general distribution of prose for the comic sub-plot and comic characters and verse for the romantic action. The King and his companions, however, speak prose quite as freely as verse, even in the romantic scenes—in which the element of burlesque enters. The formal quality of the comedy is reflected in the extensive use of rhymed verse, which may be compared in formality with the Euphuistic prose periods.

At the end of the discussion of the King's laws in I, i (the proclamation, following the convention, is in prose, although the dialogue is in verse), Costard and Dull offer an ironic prose commentary on the impossible ideal, and the scene continues in prose. Verse returns in II, i, but is broken when

5*

the Princess, instead of replying in verse to Ferdinand's
courteous verse welcome, snaps:

'Fair' I give you back again, and welcome I have not yet. The roof
of this court is too high to be yours, and welcome to the wide fields too
base to be mine. (lines 91–94)[46]

The rest of the scene is in verse. The humorous realism of
the Princess' prose contrasts markedly with the courtly for-
malities offered her.

The text of Act III is entirely in prose except for Berowne's
two speeches, one romantic and the other mock-romantic. In the brief colloquy between Berowne and Costard (in
which one regularly speaks verse and the other prose: another
indication of the play's early date) a new development in
the plot is begun, and it is made possible for the act to end
with the noble lovers again uppermost in the audience's
mind.

Act IV opens in verse, drops briefly into prose at Costard's
entrance, then returns to verse for a dozen lines (of which,
oddly enough, Costard speaks four), after which Boyet reads
Armado's second letter. The scene then alternates between
prose and a comic rhymed verse, which makes use of stichomythia. In scene ii, the pedants use artificial prose in which
to criticize the artificial verse of the two poems, establishing
an especially refined contrast. Criticism, from Hamlet's
speech to the Players to Thersites' railing, finds its medium
in prose. Whether the motive be the restoration of realism and
common sense, or the degradation of persons or ideas, the
critical impulse remains intellectual rather than emotional.

In scene iii the impassioned Berowne derides himself in
a prose soliloquy. There are various explanations for Berowne's use of prose at this point: as the most natural and
realistic of the nobles, he has a peculiar right to prose; his
mock-heroic rhetoric, were it in verse, would tire the ear
after the double dose of burlesque verse in the previous

scene; his prose offers a pleasing contrast with the torrents of verse to come, and employs the pattern and style of the Shakespearean clown *tirade*.

The first scene of Act V uses prose for the conversation of Armado and the pedants. Scene ii is in verse for almost five hundred lines (the mock-romantic episode of the disguised nobles' visit) and then goes into prose for the pageant of the Nine Worthies. Verse and prose are jumbled together, occasionally to serve some purpose (as in the set speeches of the Worthies), sometimes for more obscure reasons. The King and Berowne both have prose speeches ending in comic couplets. The nobles supply a good deal of improvised rhyming and verbal horseplay in both media. When the death of the Princess' father is announced, verse immediately becomes dominant—except for Armado's ambiguous exit-line—and the missions are delegated and oaths administered in a rather stiff and brittle verse. Armado makes a prose introduction of the final song, and adds two prose lines of epilogue.

It seems sufficiently clear that the play has nothing like a consistent alternation of prose and verse corresponding to elements in its structure. Almost all the characters are capable of speaking either prose or verse, and their choice of medium is generally dictated by the decorum of the individual scene. Thus the romantic or pseudo-romantic scenes are in verse: the qualification must be added because the form of the romantic scene is maintained even when the matter is travestied. The out-and-out clown, Costard, has the prose of his profession, except for a few odd verse lines and the set verse of "Pompey the Big." Armado, the Euphuist, speaks prose; he must remain faithful to the only medium which can display his peculiar stylistic aberration.

The nobles seem to be most comfortable in verse, although Berowne's curious prose soliloquy (IV, iii) appears to reveal something of his true nature. The manner is a bit stiff, but the matter will presently find its ablest exponent in Benedick. When the other courtiers essay prose, they are expert enough. Their criticisms of the pageant—which must recall the final scene of *A Midsummer Night's Dream*—are in a light and gay prose which gains by contrast with the Worthies' sluggish verse. And, moreover, since the discussion is critical, prose is doubly appropriate.

Shakespeare in *Love's Labour's Lost* appears relatively little concerned about his forms, except for the various poems inserted in the text. Pedants, clowns, schoolmasters, Euphuistic courtiers all speak prose because their peculiar gifts are best displayed in prose. But rhymed verse is used as well as prose for purely comic effects; comic prose has not yet come into its own in Shakespearean comedy.

2. *The Two Gentlemen of Verona*

The distribution of prose and verse in *The Two Gentlemen of Verona* (1594) follows, with a few changes, the commonest pattern of Elizabethan comedy. The romantic plot of the two gentlemen and their mistresses is in verse; the comic byplay of the masters with their servants, and particularly that between the servants, is in prose. Julia, in her boy's dress, speaks prose with the Host (IV, ii) and with Proteus (IV, iv); in the latter scene, she has but one prose line, in the dialogue with Launce. She follows Proteus' lead in returning to verse as soon as Launce leaves and the conversation grows serious.

The best prose-scenes are Launce's comic monologues and the "volleys of words" between Launce and Speed. The first volley (Proteus and Speed on love-sickness) is placed between the introductory scene of Proteus and Valentine (I, i) and the two scenes in which Julia and Proteus severally reveal their love (I, ii and iii). This exchange of witticisms,

like the similar discussion between Valentine and Speed in
II, i, has the quality of vaudeville dialogue. A theme is taken
from the serious plot and developed in rapid, fragmentary
style with many puns and verbal flights. The relevance of
these wit-combats to the main thread of the play is incon-
spicuous. Shakespeare nevertheless makes at least a token
effort to integrate this material, whereas Marlowe and Greene
frankly give it its head. But the entire device itself is lame;
it is too artificial, unspontaneous, and labored to leave the
plane of vaudeville for that of high comedy. At its best, it
takes the form of interpolated set speeches (such as Speed's
description of his love-sick master in II, i), or exchanges one
mechanical pattern for another, as in the servants' bawdy
anatomy of the milkmaid (III, i, 302 ff.), the excellence of
which consists entirely in Launce's glosses on Speed's text;
these comments relate the whole scene to the consistent strain
of humor so well represented throughout the play by Launce.

On Launce's monologue-dialogues (II, iii and IV, iv)
Shakespeare lavished the best and most artful prose in the
play. Whether or not it was improvised by the gifted comedian Kempe, it has nevertheless Shakespeare's silent sanc-
tion and may therefore be rightfully included in this discussion. Launce succeeds in making the "sourest-natured
dog" one of the most vivid characters in a play whose people,
on the whole, remain wooden and incredible. Launce is
above all an actor, with a genius for pantomime; he assigns
rôles to his dog, his shoes, his staff, and makes them all come
alive in his speech. The dog, whose function in the amorous
intrigue is palpably minor, is first the most insensitive of
creatures, who refuses to be moved while all of Launce's
family is bordering on hysterics; he later becomes the protagonist in the unsavoury but amusing episode of Silvia's
dinner, and the description of the banquet becomes unex-
pectedly vivid.

Launce parodies his master: "I have the wit to think my master is a kind of a knave," he tells us in III, i, and makes his master's love-sickness the starting-point for his account of his own love-pangs. His description is a series of antitheses and qualifications designed to excite the admiration of a Proust. And when he has once mentioned his love's "qualities," he has a list of them neatly written out, from which his comic imagination draws further inspiration.

Julia's prose in IV, ii, is the earliest instance in which prose contributes to a disguise. Her light conversation completes the illusion created first by her boy's attire. It is interesting to see that her prose here takes the form of comment on Thurio's song: criticism again, and Shakespeare's young gentlefolk are tireless critics of the arts.

Prose is, then, largely alien to the principal matter of *The Two Gentlemen of Verona*; it is chiefly restricted to clowns, and to nobles when they disport themselves with or as clowns. Another indication that this play marks an early stage in Shakespeare's use of dramatic prose is dialogue in which one character speaks prose and another verse (cf. I, ii). What should be noted is that most of the characters speak prose as easily as verse, although not so willingly; and Julia's use of prose, as noted above, introduces an element which will henceforth be encountered more frequently.

3. *A Midsummer Night's Dream*

As in *The Two Gentlemen of Verona*, prose and verse in *A Midsummer Night's Dream* (1595) fall to the comic and romantic plots respectively. In the latter play, however, there is a particular value in the distribution. In the ordinary comedy, it is the difference in atmosphere and general subject-matter which is marked off by prose and verse; Launce deals in prose, Valentine in verse, but one is not intended to believe that Launce and Valentine live in different worlds.

In *A Midsummer Night's Dream*, on the contrary, the question is in fact one of different worlds. Four concentric circles may be distinguished: the play is entirely circumscribed by the fairy world; just within is the circle of Theseus, Hippolyta and their nuptials, which establishes the temporal bounds of the play; the next circle is that of the Athenian mechanics; and the innermost is that of the four lovers, whose misadventures form the little fable of love which links all four circles.

The royal lovers and the hapless young lovers clearly have the first claim on blank verse, for their themes are the most purely romantic and lyrical of the play. Theseus and Hippolyta set the stage:

> Now, fair Hippolyta, our nuptial hour
> Draws on apace. Four happy days bring in
> Another moon...
> Four days will quickly steep themselves in night;
> Four nights will quickly dream away the time;
> And then the moon, like to a silver bow
> New-bent in heaven, shall behold the night
> Of our solemnities. (I, i, 1–3, 7–11)

And Theseus sends Philostrate forth to prepare the revels. At the very last, it will be Theseus who—as he thinks—brings the play to an end:

> Sweet friends, to bed,
> A fortnight hold we this solemnity,
> In nightly revels and new jollity. (V, i, 375–377)

But, in spite of his injunction, "Let your epilogue alone," it is Puck who provides the epilogue, appropriately making the final comment on the intrigue which he has contrived.

The fairies use blank verse as freely as do the two groups of aristocrats, but as a rule reserve it for the romantic plot of Oberon and Titania or for the Athenian lovers. They have another form of expression peculiarly suited to them, the

rhymed octosyllabic line, which has the quality of a charm or
an incantation. It is a favorite with Shakespeare, and he uses
it freely here, in *Macbeth*, in *King Lear* (for the Fool's mock
prophecy) and even in *Measure for Measure* (III, ii, 275–
296), where its ritualistic flavor conveys the sense that the
Duke is controlling all the actions of his puppets. The short,
regular line, with its recurring rhyme, has overtones of
magic and spells; in spite of its simplicity, it is capable of
much variation. Thus, when a charm is pronounced by
Oberon, one rhyme serves for all the lines:

> Flower of this purple dye,
> Hit with Cupid's archery,
> Sink in apple of his eye!
> When his love he doth espy,
> Let her shine as gloriously
> As the Venus of the sky.
> When thou wak'st, if she be by,
> Beg of her for remedy. (III, ii, 102–109).

Puck, on the other hand, sums up his search in couplets:

> Through the forest have I gone,
> But Athenian found I none
> On whose eyes I might approve
> This flower's force in stirring love... (II, ii, 66–69).

When he applies the last charm, the lines grow still shorter,
although a few octosyllabic lines are used for variety:

> On the ground
> Sleep sound.
> I'll apply
> To your eye,
> Gentle lover, remedy.
> When thou wak'st,
> Thou tak'st
> True delight
> In the sight
> Of thy former lady's eye... (III, ii, 448–457)

And yet another form, the quatrain, is exploited for the
epilogue:

> Now the hungry lion roars,
>   And the wolf behowls the moon;
> Whilst the heavy ploughman snores,
>   All with weary task fordone... (V, i, 378–381)

These are the forms that the fairies employ. When they essay
blank verse, their accents are yet unmistakeable:

> What hempen homespuns have we swagg'ring here,
> So near the cradle of the Fairy Queen?
> What, a play toward? I'll be an auditor;
> An actor too perhaps, if I see cause. (III, i, 79–82)

Nor is Oberon's lyricism easily confused with that of Theseus.

The "hempen homespuns" are prose speakers; for that
reason, among others, their verse play is richly humorous.
The bastard verse of *Pyramus and Thisbe* is the only verse
these men could possibly speak, just as a burlesque of *Romeo
and Juliet* is the only love-tragedy they could possibly play.
Their prose is good, simple, direct. The Moon, too long
provoked, sheds his verse like a heavy coat and speaks his
mind:

> All that I have to say is to tell you that the lanthorn is the moon; I,
> the man i' the moon this; thorn-bush, my thorn-bush; and this dog,
> my dog. (V, i, 261–264)

When poetry fails to achieve the desired effect or to convey
the desired meaning, this jewel of critics will have none of it.
Bottom too is a critic; here he deals with the theory of acting:

> Nay, you must name his name, and half his face must be seen
> through the lion's neck, and he himself must speak through, saying thus,
> or to the same defect: 'Ladies,'—or 'Fair ladies,—I would wish you'
> —or 'I would request you'—or 'I would entreat you—not to fear,
> not to tremble. My life for yours! If you think I come hither as a lion,
> it were pity of my life. No! I am no such thing. I am a man as other
> men are.' And there, indeed, let him name his name and tell them
> plainly he is Snug the joiner. (III, i, 37–47)

Such is the mechanics' prose, in the mouth of Bottom, their
virtuoso.

To this point, the distribution of prose and verse follows
the lines of character alone. Sufficient contrast is obtained
by the opposition of various kinds of verse to make the contrast between verse and prose insignificant. The first rehears-
al scene (III, i) brings in burlesque verse briefly for Bottom's exit and reappearance with the ass's head. When Bottom wakes Titania with his song, she speaks verse to his prose
throughout their short-lived amour. In the reunion of the
mechanics (IV, ii), the clowns reveal themselves as the per-
petuators of a tradition:

> *Quince.* It is not possible. You have not a man in all Athens
> able to discharge Pyramus but he.
> *Flute.* No, he hath simply the best wit of any handicraft man in
> Athens.
> *Quince.* Yea, and the best person too, and he is a very paramour
> for a sweet voice.
> *Flute.* You must say 'paragon.' A paramour is (God bless us!)
> a thing of naught. (IV, ii, 7–14)

"Your old vice still — mistake the word." This "trick of
the old rage" never entirely deserts Shakespeare, but his
clowns gradually discard this badge of their profession.

The mingling of prose and verse in the last scene is,
for delicacy and skill, unmatched in Shakespeare's work.
It begins with Theseus' exquisite speech on the lunatic, the
lover, and the poet, which not only sums up the previous
action but also provides an ironic commentary on *Pyramus
and Thisbe*, that fine flowering of the poetic imagination
which is shortly to divert the company. After Quince has
rid his prologue "like a rough colt," Theseus and the rest—
none of whom has previously spoken prose—begin a barrage of quips and puns in prose. Their remarks are witty;
but, after all, they have a splendid text to annotate. At least
once they soar above mere mockery:

Hippolyta. This is the silliest stuff that ever I heard.

Theseus. The best in this kind are but shadows; and the worst are no worse, if imagination amend them.

Hippolyta. It must be your imagination then, and not theirs.

Theseus. If we imagine no worse of them than they of themselves, they may pass for excellent men. Here come two noble beasts in, a man and a lion. (V, i, 213–221)

Technically, at least, this is critical prose; and the form is doubly appropriate. The speakers have not hitherto dealt with such a theme; and their remarks offer a delightful contrast with the extraordinary verse. The prose follows a quite rigid form; any of the characters—with the exception quoted above—might speak any of the lines. One may here confound Theseus' prose with Lysander's, although their verse is clearly distinguishable.

Theseus' final verse speech is clearly intended, as far as he is concerned, to close the play. The entrance of Puck, bound on purely elvish tasks, prepares the fairy masque which actually brings the play to an end. He and his troop speak the short verse of charms and enchantments, and the magical note is the last to be heard. Puck can without a break retain the same meter for his epilogue.

So prose comes into its own in the final scene and performs its function of contrast. The quantity of prose in the play and the ways in which it is used are limited, because the play is rich in a multiplicity of form of expression, and also because the play's inspiration does not require or permit a wider use of prose. Although *A Midsummer Night's Dream* shows no great stylistic or dramatic advance in the use of prose, in no other play are prose and the several forms of verse so skillfully blended.

4. *The Taming of the Shrew*

The arrangement of prose and verse in *The Taming of the Shrew* (?1596) is normal for Shakespeare's early plays; of two characters in a single scene, one may regularly speak prose, and the other verse. Shakespeare invests this rigid pattern with a new life, and, although he is not to exercise his full command over this device until later in his career, he employs it to good advantage in this play.

The prose dialogue of Christopher Sly and the Hostess opens the Induction. The entrance of the Lord, the servants, and players brings verse. When Sly awakens in the Lord's bedchamber, he speaks prose *until* he is persuaded that, as a lord, he has actually slept fifteen years in his delirium. At this point, he assumes his imagined position and speaks verse:

> Am I a lord? and have I such a lady?
> Or do I dream? or have I dream'd till now?
> I do not sleep: I see, I hear, I speak;
> I smell sweet savours and I feel soft things.
> Upon my life, I am a lord indeed,
> And not a tinker, nor Christophero Sly.
> Well, bring our lady hither to our sight,
> And once again a pot o' the smallest ale. (Induction, ii, 70–77)

Sly's last speeches in the Induction (after his new-found wife has postponed the consummation of their marriage) are again in prose, the first comments on the play to be performed. When he again speaks, at the end of I, i, his prose may signify a reversion to character or merely comic byplay. This interplay of prose and verse in the Induction shows no little subtlety; against the rough prose which Sly has hitherto used (itself effectively contrasted with the innocuous verse of the Lord and servants) is set his new, bombastic, and unmistakable verse, accompanied by elaborate stage-business.

A more primitive prose-verse distribution may be seen in I, ii, where Grumio, after speaking a few comic couplets with Petruchio, speaks only prose to the verse of Petruchio and Hortensio. He offers a satirical commentary on the serious dialogue, ranging from long outbursts to the clown's familiar one-line asides. The clown's burlesque function is reduced in this play to such incidental comment, as the comic action is here the principal plot.

Prose does not, on the whole, play a very important part; at least once, in III, i, it is used only because verse would be quite impossible. Lucentio and Bianca speak prose when they pretend to construe the Latin verses, because it would obviously tax any poet's powers to make poetry of such broken matter; moreover, Shakespeare is parodying the form of a typical schoolboy's recitation. The scene has been in verse to this point, and returns to verse immediately following this episode.

Petruchio conducts his taming chiefly in verse, but descriptions of him and of his actions are generally in prose. Thus Biondello:

Why, Petruchio is coming—in a new hat and an old jerkin; a pair of old breeches thrice turn'd; a pair of boots that have been candle-cases, one buckled, another lac'd; an old rusty sword ta'en out of the town arm oury, with a broken hilt, and chapeless; with two broken points; his horse hipp'd, with an old mothy saddle and stirrups of no kindred; besides possess'd with the glanders and like to mose in the chine, troubled with the lampass, infected with the fashions, full of windgalls, sped with spavins, rayed with the yellows, past cure of the fives, stark spoil'd with the staggers... (III, ii, 43–56)

This is not Shakespeare's familiar comic prose style; it is a kind of Rabelaisian huddling of jest upon jest and word upon word. Petruchio's portrait is painted, and, as the cream of the jest, the subject himself appears and far exceeds expectations. Prose is used for a similar exposition- and preparation-scene in IV, i, where Grumio tells Curtis of the indignities which Petruchio has heaped on Katherine, whereupon the two enter and beggar Grumio's account of them. In this way, the prose exposition-scene is given an uncommon turn, which will become a familiar device in Shakespeare's work.

5. *The Merchant of Venice*

The Merchant of Venice (1596) introduces a new kind of prose, but also employs every kind of prose that Shakespeare has until now found useful. For it has Launcelot Gobbo's clown-scenes, and speeches; the light banter of Portia and Nerissa (I, ii), which looks back to the courtly badinage of the nobles in *Love's Labour's Lost* and forward to the dialogues of Rosalind and Orlando; the conventional prose of Bellario's letter to the Duke (IV, i); and, most important, the prose of Shylock.

The most obvious fact about Shylock—and neither he nor anyone else in the play hesitates to state it again and again—is that he has nothing whatever to do with the world in which we see him. To this end, every difference between him and his Christian enemies is dwelt upon: his person, his voice, his customs and manners, his character. When he comes on the scene, his very presence is a harsh and alien element in a world which is otherwise compounded of sweet sounds and sights. The monstrousness is in the contrast rather than in Shylock himself. Mark Van Doren has very justly said of him:

> Yet Shylock is not a monster. He is a man thrust into a world bound not to endure him. In such a world he necessarily looks and sounds ugly. In another universe his voice might have its properties and its uses. Here it can issue as nothing but a snarl, an animal cry sounding outrageously among the flute and recorder voices of persons whose very names, unlike his own, are flowing musical phrases. The contrast between harmony and hate, love and discord, is here complete, and Shakespeare for the time being is content to resolve it in comedy. Even in his tragedies it cannot be more complete[47].

By its very nature, drama, and particularly poetic drama, tells us of men and women by making them express their minds and characters in their voices. Shakespeare summarizes all the interloper in Shylock in that "snarl."

What distinguishes the style of Shylock is in the end, no doubt, one of its author's secrets. But we can hear the difference between him and the brethren of Antonio. And in the quality of that difference we should have no difficulty in recognizing Shylock as the alien element in a world of love and friendship, of nightingales and moonlight sleeping sweetly on a bank.[48]

When Shylock enters for the first time, in I, iii, he is discussing the loan—in clipped and businesslike prose—with Bassanio. Shylock breaks into a sarcastic eulogy of Antonio's financial situation, listing the perils that beset merchants, and, a moment later, violently rejects Bassanio's dinner invitation. There is a suppressed fury in his words which breaks out in his second speech, a string of short, bitter phrases. At Antonio's entrance, Shylock exposes his hatred in a brief verse aside, and the scene continues in verse. The matter-of-fact tone of the earlier dialogue is discarded for a rather sententious verse, in which Biblical quotations are embedded. This verse is then exchanged for the passionate verse in which Shylock and Antonio frankly reveal themselves. Shylock returns to a mocking, friendly tone for his adieux.

Shylock speaks prose in one other crucial scene. The scurrilous Solanio and Salerio set the stage in III, i, in prose, and Shylock retains the form when he enters. The Jew and Christians exchange curses, and Shylock breaks into his great tirade. His prose is desperate and fevered; if it be an outgrowth of clown prose, then the clownishness is surely in the attitude of his auditors and hardly in the speech itself. His subject is "worthy" of verse, but his passion will not suffer itself to be contained in more rigid forms; his words jostle each other in their haste to be forth. The fury and sincerity of his utterance contrast with the casual tone which Antonio's friends so easily employ in speaking of either Antonio's or Shylock's misfortunes. There is nothing casual about Shylock; his passions encompass his destruction.

Launcelot Gobbo's best and longest scene (II, ii) shows him to be a lineal descendant of Launce and an adept exponent of the latter's style. Inanimate objects are not, as in Launce's speeches, assigned parts; instead, Launcelot's conscience and the devil speak with most miraculous organ. This speech is one of Shakespeare's most effective clownmonologues, and departs somewhat from the classic form; the father, Old Gobbo, is made the butt of a mildly brutal deception. (Edgar and Gloucester are to find other uses for this material.) The clown-scene is well integrated with the principal plot.

The first four acts of *The Merchant of Venice* display an almost mechanical alternation of prose and verse. I, i, which prepares the action, is entirely in verse except for the half-dozen lines in which Bassanio criticizes Gratiano. Scene ii shows Portia and Nerissa in light prose conversation. Scene iii opens with the prose of Shylock and Bassanio and passes into verse, as observed above. II, i, is the verse-scene of Portia and Morocco. Scene ii is the prose-scene of the Gobbos, which gives way to the verse of Bassanio and Gratiano. The short scenes of the remainder of the act, which advance the various amorous intrigues, are all in verse, except for Launcelot's brief speeches. III, i, is the long prose-scene of Shylock, Tubal and the tormentors. Scene ii depicts the winning of Portia; only Antonio's letter is in prose. Scenes iii and iv are in verse: the first shows an obdurate Shylock; the second, Portia preparing for the trial. Scene v, which is rather longer, begins with a comic prose dialogue between Jessica and Launcelot, continues in prose after Lorenzo's entrance, and ends in verse after the clown leaves. Bellario's letter appears as a unique prose passage in Act IV, where the solemn atmosphere of the court imposes verse.

From this point forward conflict disappears from the play, and with it the necessity for formal contrast. Launcelot has two or three lines of prose in V, i, but they are the last. Music and order have been restored to the world of Belmont, and time is passed in the exquisitely patterned love-making of Lorenzo and Jessica, and the mock-quarrel of the wives and husbands. Prose would be as inappropriate in this atmosphere as Shylock himself.

Shylock's prose marks Shakespeare's most daring and original use of the medium to this point in his development. It is poignant and impassioned, and its harshness and discord introduce a painful realism. Shylock's insistent questions evoke mocking replies from his enemies, but they leave us a brilliant and disturbing portrait. Prose in Shylock's vein will henceforth be encountered more often in tragedy than in comedy; but *The Merchant of Venice* has itself often been read and played as tragedy.

6. Henry IV

Nowhere in Shakespeare are the boundaries of two worlds so clearly delimited by the use of prose and verse as in the *Henry IV* plays (1597, 1598). The scenes relating to the historical matter are in verse, the scenes of Falstaff and his followers in prose. There are trifling exceptions: the conventional usages, as in Hotspur's letter (II, iii); Hotspur's short comic dialogue with his lady (III, i), with its startling shifts between prose and verse; and the mock verse of Pistol. One can hardly say of plays which fall so neatly into two actions and two spheres of influence that the form of either action is basic and the form of the other is the exception. Between the two worlds lies a huge and fundamental opposition, but each is autonomous within itself; Pistol's verse in the Boar's Head tavern is burlesque, not a sadly distorted recollection that the "serious business" of the play is going on elsewhere in verse.

Falstaff is Shakespeare's most brilliant speaker of comic

prose, as Hamlet is his most gifted speaker of a prose which defies categories. But why does Falstaff speak prose? This may seem an idle question: Falstaff is a clown, although a nobleman, and must therefore speak prose; he must, furthermore, represent "the whole world" that Hal has to banish before he can become England's Harry, and Falstaff must therefore be opposed in every conceivable way to the world of high action and noble verse in which Hal is destined to move. But beyond all this, Falstaff speaks prose because it is inconceivable that he should speak anything else. He is the incarnation of realism, who, in George Orwell's words, "sees very clearly the advantages of staying alive with a whole skin ... He it is who punctures your fine attitudes and urges you to look after Number One, to be unfaithful to your wife, to bilk your debts, and so on and so forth."[49] He is the soldier who carries, not unlike Bernard Shaw's Bluntschli, a bottle of sack in his holster, and who remains on the battlefield to question the meaning of honor after the rest have gone forth to seek it. Verse in his mouth is but a mockery of verse, and as such he speaks it. Prose in Shakespeare's earlier chronicle-histories has been the rough speech of Jack Cade and his ragamuffins. Falstaff's prose is the very honey of Hybla. The devil may speak through him, but such is his utterance that the angels are easily worsted.

Burlesque lies near the heart of Shakespearean comedy, from *The Comedy of Errors* to *As You Like It*. In the two *Henry IV* plays, the Falstaff-plot offers the broadest conceivable burlesque on the serious action. Falstaff derides the chivalric ideal, the forms of noble behavior, the law itself; he robs the travelers, suffers himself to be robbed in turn without fighting, and at last lies grossly and complacently about the whole affair and is totally unabashed at being found out. He is an unrepentant sinner, and, notwithstanding, is handsomely rewarded for his evil life until the moment of his banishment. He is a particularly noisome stench in the nostrils of the godly. His burlesque of their world is conducted on every plane: he robs them, flouts their ideals, and corrupts their prince. And, because he is in such constant opposition to their world, it is only fitting that he should never really speak its language. The powerful contrast is expressed on the level of speech as on every other, and thus Falstaff speaks prose because of what he represents as well as what he is.

Most of the characters can be assigned easily enough to one group or the other—Hal's position remaining always ambiguous—but Hotspur's case is somewhat odd. He accepts the code completely; he is honor's fool, and is killed for it. But he is a very downright man, whose hard and realistic common sense makes him impatient with both poetry and milk-and-water oaths; language must speak clearly, directly, and forcefully, or he will have none of it. It is therefore inevitable that he should speak the very best of language, and that especially in verse. His verse is so hard, colloquial, and simple that he really has no need for prose. George Rylands says that Hotspur's speech marks an important stage in the development of Shakespeare's verse style, a stage at which Shakespeare incorporated into his verse many of the qualities of his prose.[50] And yet one feels that Shakespeare must have known what he was about when he made Hotspur speak much more verse than prose. Hotspur belongs, after all, to the world of the knights, and he must speak their idiom even if only to mock them in it. Occasionally he uses prose, and very well, as in the prose letter in II, iii—a furious stream of prose: letter, comment, and vituperation, all well jumbled together. But as soon as Lady Percy enters, we have verse dialogue. The prose of this first long monologue should perhaps be put down to a combination of conventional epistolary prose and the dramatic necessity for continuing the letter scene in prose, even after the reading of the letter is finished.

In III, i, where Hotspur taunts and enrages the fiery Glendower, he begins in broken verse:

> Lord Mortimer, and cousin Glendower,
> Will you sit down?
> And uncle Worcester. A plague upon it!
> I have forgot the map. (III, i, 3–5)

Glendower's reply has been rearranged as most irregular verse by Pope from the prose of the Quartos. Hotspur's next speech is in prose, whereas Glendower at once breaks into the pompous, inflated verse so characteristic of him. Hotspur then varies between prose and verse; the length of the individual speech appears to be the only determinant. Thus he says at first:

Why, so it would have done at the same season, if your mother's cat had but kitten'd, though yourself had never been born. (18–20).

But, a moment later, he goes on:

> And I say the earth was not of my mind,
> If you suppose as fearing you it shook.
> . . . .
> O, then the earth shook to see the heavens on fire,
> And not in fear of your nativity.
> Diseased nature oftentimes breaks forth
> In strange eruptions; oft the teeming earth
> Is with a kind of colic pinch'd and vex'd
> By the imprisoning of unruly wind
> Within her womb, which, for enlargement striving,
> Shakes the old beldame earth and topples down
> Steeples and mossgrown towers. At your birth
> Our grandam earth, having this distemp'rature,
> In passion shook. (22–23, 25–34)

After Glendower's reply, Hotspur returns to prose for a two-line retort, and, a little later, speaks verse again. Hotspur's prose in this scene appears to be restricted to short gibes, whereas he speaks verse when he becomes aroused.

He uses prose again, briefly, toward the end of the scene, when he jokes with his wife and reproaches her for her genteel swearing. It is difficult to assign any specific reason for this prose, largely because of the general uncertainty of media in this passage (227–265). Hotspur speaks prose, then verse, then prose again; after the Welsh lady's song, Hotspur's protest against his lady's "in good sooth" begins in prose and drops suddenly into verse. His last speech is again in prose. The Quartos and Folio disagree on the setting of the mixed speech. The Quartos have

> Not yours, in good sooth? Heart! you swear like a comfit-maker's wife. 'Not you, in good sooth!' and 'as true as I live!' and 'as God shall mend me!' and 'as sure as day!'
> And givest such sarcenet surety for thy oaths
> As if thou ne'er walk'st further than Finsbury,
> Swear me, Kate, like a lady as thou art,
> A good mouth-filling oath; and leave 'in sooth'
> And such protest of pepper gingerbread
> To velvet guards and Sunday citizens.
> Come, sing. (250–260)

which is the form generally accepted by modern editors. The Folios, however, make verse of lines 250–253, ending the lines at *sooth?*, *wife*, *live*, and *day*. The Quartos are doubtless correct in their reading; but one's confusion finds honorable precedents.

The Prince, in general, takes his cue from his company, speaking prose in the tavern and verse in the court with equal facility. His one violation of this division is, consequently, all the more striking. He enters in V, iii, to find Falstaff moralizing over the corpse of Sir Walter Blunt. Hal is now no longer the boon companion, but the valiant knight, and reproves Falstaff in straightforward verse. Falstaff replies with a jest in prose, and the rest of the scene— a matter of a half-dozen speeches—is wound up in prose. But Falstaff himself has brought his prose into a verse scene, one of noble words and deeds, and he has used Sir Walter's "grinning honour" as a telling proof of his conclusions in his own catechism of honor. The scene thus contains a double contrast between prose and verse, and the old use of prose and verse characters within a single scene is here given a new and effective turn.

In V, i, Falstaff is for the first time brought into the world of the court, and at once sets about his favorite task of deriding it. Worcester pleads his innocence, and to the King's ironic question about the rebellion, "You have not sought it! How comes it then?" (V, i, 27), Falstaff interjects a reply: "Rebellion lay in his way, and he found it." Only Hal's injunction to remain quiet keeps Falstaff from making further comments on the action of the scene. He must needs hold his peace until the nobles have left, but immediately thereafter rediscovers his vein. Hal is short with him, for he is keenly aware of the seriousness of the situation. And so Falstaff must wait for even Hal to leave before he can make his most devastating comment on the ideals of a world he so ambiguously serves.

Shakespeare was too keen a dramatist not to have understood that the most powerful impression a scene creates in the mind of an audience is the final one. The first scene of Act V begins with King Henry, Worcester and the rest; but it ends with Falstaff. The *dramatic* point of the scene is well made and the main action is appreciably advanced. But at the side, and attempting always to intrude, is Falstaff, and when the rest have left, he has the stage entirely to himself. The net effect is produced not by the heroics of the nobles, but by the cynical realism of Falstaff. This is not to say that Falstaff dominates the play as he dominates this scene; as Professor Van Doren has well expressed it: "History is enlarged here to make room for taverns and trollops and potations of sack, and the heroic drama is modified by gigantic mockery, by the roared voice of truth; but the result is more rather than less reality, just as a cathedral, instead of being demolished by merriment among its aisles, stands more august."[51]

Hal must, as he says, "imitate the sun," and Falstaff's charm must be made so great as to convince the spectator that Hal's enjoyment of low life is not caused by a natural preference for the stew or the alehouse. But so charming (to use the word strictly) is Falstaff that Hal's necessary renunciation of him cannot be anything but priggish. The more obvious viciousness of Falstaff's actions in *2 Henry IV* is an indication that Shakespeare was obliged to degrade deliberately the tempter who had succeeded only too well. The damage, as far as the reader or spectator is concerned, is past repair.

The striking cleavage between the two actions in *Henry IV* expresses itself in the fact that most of the scenes are entirely in prose or in verse. The exceptions in *1 Henry IV* have already been noted; they are the scenes which center around Hotspur and the two scenes of Falstaff at war. There is also the tavern scene, II, iv, which has the verse interlude of the Sheriff and Carrier, a matter of twenty lines in which Hal assumes the verse expected of him in order to get rid of Falstaff's pursuers. In *2 Henry IV* there are even fewer mixed scenes. Pistol and his mock blank verse aside, there are only three scenes—II, iv; IV, iii; and V, v—where one finds any significant bulk of both prose and verse. This fact is of interest: it helps to indicate that the gap is growing wider. Hal and Falstaff are together in only two scenes. One is the early scene in the tavern (II, iv), and the other shows Hal banishing Falstaff forever. In II, ii, Poins reads Hal the letter from Falstaff, and it seems oddly appropriate that Falstaff should speak through the mouth of his chief rival for Hal's affections and cause Hal to prepare the last trick he will play on Falstaff. During the greater part of the play, Falstaff is away in Gloucestershire pressing the miserable yokels or in the company of Prince John, "this same young sober-blooded boy" who "doth not love me." Meanwhile Hal is growing more conscious of his impending responsibilities and is learning how to live without his evil angel. In this Second Part there is a new heartless quality in his jests about Falstaff; all things combine to prepare the fat knight's downfall.

In spite of Falstaff's absence from London, the plot which he dominates throughout is closely linked to the serious action. The relevance of his association with Prince John is obvious, as is the pressing of the soldiers. His encounter with Coleville of the Dale is a sardonic comment on the superiority of reputation to fact; and yet the deceit by which Coleville comes to yield to Falstaff is less reprehensible than the one Prince John practices on Hastings and the Archbishop. Whether so direct a comparison is intended is difficult to say; but, given the burlesque nature of so much of Falstaff's part, the interpretation is certainly possible.

The alternation of all-prose and all-verse scenes in the Second Part is almost mathematical, as can be clearly seen when the play is outlined: Prologue–verse; I, i–verse; I, ii–prose; I, iii–verse; II, i–prose; II, ii–prose; II, iii–verse; II, iv–prose (with some verse); III, i–verse; III, ii–prose; IV, i–verse; IV, ii–verse; IV, iii–prose (with some verse); IV, iv–verse; IV, v–verse; V, i–prose; V, ii–verse; V, iii–prose; V, iv–prose; V, v–prose, verse, prose, verse; Epilogue —prose. Where two consecutive scenes in the same medium occur, it generally means that the same action continues with but a slight interruption (e. g., IV, i and ii; IV, iv and v). (An exception must be noted in II, i and ii, where the scene between Falstaff and the Lord Chief Justice is followed by the scene of Hal and Poins.) The play's high degree of regularity emphasizes the separation of the actions.

The most notable new verse speaker is, of course, Pistol. In his unparalleled fustian he effectively sums up what Shakespeare has to say about the old, ranting blank verse— which, to be sure, the poet had himself been known to use. But the projection of the bombastic ancient into the prose company ruled by Falstaff serves a particular end. The Quartos and Folios almost invariably print Pistol's speeches as prose. It was Pope who first printed them as the verse which they obviously are. The confusion is a natural one, for not all Pistol's speeches are verse; and those which are in verse do not always so proclaim themselves by their infallible regularity of scansion. Such a speech as

> These be good humours indeed. Shall packhorses
> And hollow pamper'd jades of Asia,
> Which cannot go but thirty mile a day,
> Compare with Cæsars, and with Cannibals,
> And Troyan Greeks? Nay, rather damn them with
> King Cerberus and let the welkin roar!
> Shall we fall foul for toys? (II, iv, 177–183)

illustrates abundantly the dilemma of the editors. But the burlesque of Marlowe in this passage gives sufficient support for setting the lines as verse.

Pistol's verse stands as an odd landmark in Shakespeare's development; verse has so long been the normal language of the Shakespearean drama that one is startled to find verse used as part of a burlesque conception of a character. For the contrast is not only between Pistol's noisy and senseless verse and the prose in which Falstaff proclaims his relation to the world, but between this intolerably stagy and preposterous verse and the wonderfully realistic verse of Hotspur. Although prose is accorded an ever greater and more important share in Shakespeare's plays, it must always be

remembered that verse, as spoken by Hotspur and Faul-
conbridge the Bastard, is finding a new vigor, and, above
all, is acquiring qualities which had previously been restricted to prose. It can hardly be determined whether
Shakespeare was actually aware that he was plundering one
medium to enrich the other (as Rylands maintains) or whether he merely felt that his conception of a Hotspur required
a verse that was somehow different, more flexible and colloquial than any he had previously used. One cannot believe
that this ever became a conscious problem in Shakespeare's
mind. Hotspur's verse is indeed the beginning of a new
time; and the old, fittingly enough, is reduced to a clown's
device. No outworn mode ever died an honorable death in
the Elizabethan theatre; "Go by, Hieronimo!" was shouted
by Jonson's clowns even before *The Spanish Tragedie* had
disappeared from the boards.

In *2 Henry IV* there is no one who can speak a blank verse
like Hotspur's to compete with Falstaff's prose. The ordinary verse is noble, dignified, and occasionally moving, as
in the King's death-bed scene; but it can hardly be said to
have the fiery, colloquial, yet withal highly poetic quality
of the best verse in the First Part. Verse and prose do not
meet as peers, as becomes strikingly evident in the introduction of Pistol's bombast. Nor is this bombast received
tolerantly: it is thrust downstairs at the point of Falstaff's
sword.

Two mixed scenes remain to be examined. The first, IV,
iii, opens with Falstaff's capture of Coleville of the Dale.
It is not quite clear why Coleville ("a famous rebel") should
permit himself to be taken so easily by the fat knight; he says
simply, "I think you are Sir John Falstaff, and in that
thought yield me." (IV, iii, 18-19). Presumably Falstaff's
calm appropriation of the honors for Hotspur's killing has
inspired "that thought." The entire episode, with Falstaff's

insistent self-glorification before Prince John, is splendid
mockery; Falstaff's false reputation brings him effortless
victory, and even earns him Prince John's good report:

> I, in my condition,
> Shall better speak of you than you deserve. (IV, iii, 90–91)

Perhaps, too, Falstaff's bloodless capture is a parody of Prince
John's own sinister triumph.

Prince John, at his entrance with his followers, brings
verse to the scene, even for his tame jesting with Falstaff.
As soon as Falstaff speaks, however, the Prince joins him in
using prose. Coleville's single long speech is in verse, as he
berates bitterly the errors of his leaders. Towards the end
of the dialogue, Falstaff speaks three lines in verse, his longest speech in that medium:

> My lord, I beseech you give me leave to go
> Through Gloucestershire; and when you come to court,
> Stand my good lord, pray, in your good report. (87–89)

It is poor enough verse. Why does he use it? He has until
now not hesitated to use prose to John. He is in all probabil-
ity consciously adopting the Prince's mode of speech in order to beg an unaccustomed favor of him. Falstaff has not
always been so solicitous of others' good reports of him. But
now he has been long absent from London and from Hal,
the King is ill, and all things are possible. As long as Falstaff can exercise his wit and charm, he has no need of the
good offices of others. These lines express not foreboding
but a sort of dramatic irony. If Falstaff were now himself
to return to London, instead of proceeding to Gloucestershire for the fleecing of Justice Shallow, he might reassert
his ancient influence over Hal in time to forestall his banishment. But his greed—and perhaps his overconfidence in
human nature—lead him astray. John once gone, Falstaff
cheerfully belabors him in his best prose and goes on to

discourse on sherris-sack. The scene ends with Falstaff, as usual, in command.

The last mixed scene is the final scene of the play. It opens with a few lines of routine prose spoken by the Grooms who strew rushes on the ground in preparation for the King's coming. They go off, and the King and his retinue pass over the stage, followed by Falstaff and his company. The latter remain, and converse in prose broken only by Pistol's account of Doll's plight:

> My knight, I will inflame thy noble liver
> And make thee rage.
> Thy Doll, and Helen of thy noble thoughts,
> Is in base durance and contagious prison,
> Hal'd thither
> By most mechanical and dirty hand.
> Rouse up revenge from ebon den with fell Alecto's snake,
> For Doll is in. Pistol speaks naught but truth. (V, v, 33–40)

Falstaff, in calm expectation of the power which is to be his, replies only, "I will deliver her." Pistol's speech has a peculiar effectiveness: its familiar pompousness is a foreshadowing of the degree and honor which all the Falstaff-party anticipates; in Doll's imprisonment we have a premonition of a general catastrophe. The speech is extraordinarily well contrived. The first seven lines thunder and bellow their way along with many high-sounding phrases; the last line lets them all down with "For Doll is in." The introduction of the short and slangy phrase produces much the effect of Max Beerbohm's *Savonarola*, in which completely banal and common words are juxtaposed with pompous and overblown terms. Falstaff's reply, short and pregnant as it is, is in the grand style; he is carrying on Pistol's manner. Only the new King can destroy this vein.

The encounter with the former Prince is, fittingly, in verse, doubly symbolizing Hal's regeneration and his assumption of his proper place in the changed order of things.

No hint of the witty prose-speaker of other times leavens the harsh and dry verse. King Henry has banished not only Falstaff but Prince Hal.

The prose of Falstaff's dialogue with Shallow is brave but brief; Prince John and the Lord Chief Justice dispose of it permanently. The play ends with their verse conversation, and, although John touches briefly on Falstaff, his eye is already on the future. This is the note that prevails as the play comes to its conclusion, nor is it altered by the prose Epilogue, a set speech of a familiar order which is an apology for the play that is past and a prospectus for the one to come. The prose is mannered and nicely balanced, and has a rhetorical, undramatic movement. The dancer adroitly and wittily makes capital of his profession. Much as the Epilogue resembles Rosalind's, the latter is more akin to Shakespeare's dramatic prose and consequently more effective.

7. Henry V

Henry IV uses prose and verse to mark off the limits of two antagonistic worlds; Henry V (1600) makes a less profound but more diverse use of prose, because the imperial party has triumphed and now seeks an opponent on its own level. No Falstaff holds sway in prose, rallying around him all those of his persuasion and speech. In Henry V prose is spoken, for a great variety of reasons, by Bardolph, Nym, Dame Quickly, King Henry, Fluellen, and the French; but the dominant speech is always the heroic blank verse. Prose is again subordinated, in spite of its considerable bulk, to its ancient function, that of the intruder. The King uses it freely and expertly, but he has lost his old art, and the play's prose, as a whole, rises to its old heights only (as one might guess) in the Hostess' account of Falstaff's death.

Certain of the scenes, e.g., II,i; II,iii; and III,ii, are comic scenes in the old manner and therefore in prose. Shakespeare returns to old and tried humorous material with Fluellen, Macmorris, and Captain Jamy; as comic characters, they would in any case require prose, but as dialect comedians, they have another and even more urgent reason. Henry Sharpe listed broken English as one of the causes for the use of prose,[52] and although one hesitates to establish a special category, Sharpe was not without a certain justification. Some Elizabethan playwrights, such as Marston, went so far as to confect blank verse in broken English, but Shakespeare refused to deal in such macaronic nonsense. The irregularity of broken English renders it incapable of supporting the demands of verse; a language in which one constantly hesitates and stumbles is not an idiom for poetry. For the same reason—and because the scenes are comic—Henry and Katherine's polyglot lovemaking (V, ii) and Katherine's English lesson (III, iv) are in prose.

Pistol continues, in this play, to speak his peculiar verse, which again offers a contrast to the prose of the other comic characters. But the nature of that contrast has meanwhile changed. Whereas Pistol was set off against Falstaff in *2 Henry IV*, and his verse represented an intrusion on Falstaff's world, he is now compared with another *miles gloriosus*, Nym. The bladders of wind belabor each other, one in prose and the other in verse, and their conflict is meaningless, except in that it prepares Fluellen's eventual outfacing of Pistol. Pistol and his company were at best an inglorious crew when Falstaff led them; but in *Henry V* they undergo steady degradation. Pistol might have turned bawd in *Henry IV*; but he would hardly have announced it so complacently.

As in *Henry IV*, the mixed scenes are few, but of more than passing interest, centering chiefly around the character of the King. In III, vi, after Pistol and Fluellen's low comedy (in which the former's rant is contrasted with the sober and dull moralizing of the model man-at-arms), the King enters and converses with Fluellen in the prose of a soldier in the field. To him comes Montjoy, short and blunt of speech, and delivers his message in the plainest prose of the play. The King's reply is in a proud, handsome verse. On this note, mingled with a reasonable piety, the scene ends. Against it is juxtaposed scene vii, in the French camp, which shows Orléans, the Dauphin, and the Constable in a light and mannered prose conversation which would seem more appropriate in Lyly's *Endimion* than on the eve of Agincourt. This frivolity, expressed in short, punning quips and ripostes, offers an almost crude contrast with the solemn note of dedication in Henry's verse.

The series of encounters between the disguised King and Pistol, Bates, Williams, and the rest occasions the most striking use of prose in the play. The King takes Sir Thomas Erpingham's cloak after a short verse conversation and remains alone on the stage. Pistol enters and addresses him in his usual verse, to which the King replies in one- or two-line prose speeches. After Pistol's exit, the King listens, unobserved, to the dialogue of Gower and Fluellen, on which he comments in verse. The scene rises to its height with the entrance of Bates, Court, and Williams, who speak to the King in prose; he replies in the same form, in his disguise of a common soldier. His prose is sober, except for a few quibbles in the earlier speeches, where Shakespeare cannot resist playing on the irony of having the King discuss himself; later in the colloquy, the King's tone becomes quite evangelical, and he so far forgets his assumed character as to deliver a heated sermon on the mutual responsibilities of the King and his soldiers. The men are not disabused, because of the dramatic necessities involved, although they might well grow suspicious of so fluent an apologist. The long speech gives way to a rapid exchange of short speeches and gages. When the soldiers have left, Henry returns at once to his usual verse for the long speech on ceremony. He will not again use prose until the battle is won and he is joking with Williams and Fluellen on the battlefield. In the scene of Williams' encounter with Fluellen (IV, viii), the King, even in his jesting, remains *au-dessus de la mêlée* and speaks only verse with the combatants.

The last scene of the play, V, ii, presents in verse the final reconciliation of the French and English. Henry and Katherine are then left together on the stage for the wooing, which the King begins in verse. At her first protest, he promptly shifts to prose and his speeches grow ever longer, until he seems to be battering her with words rather than courting her. Perhaps it was intended that Katherine's faulty speaking of her own tongue should go unnoticed in the cascade of Henry's speeches; his own incompetence in French is dramatically necessary and altogether plausible.

When the French reënter, the comic note is still dominant; Burgundy begins in verse, but soon breaks off. At the end of the marriage discussion, when the terms of the treaty are mentioned, verse returns except for Exeter's single prose speech, in which he quotes the formulae to be used in addressing Henry. These, having the effect of a proclamation or any other such document, quite naturally go into prose; and the whole speech, by sympathy, goes into that form.

Henry V uses prose fairly lavishly, not only for clowns, but for the light and almost Euphuistic conversation of warriors whose pretensions are greater than their abilities; to assist in disguising a King by lending him a foot-soldier's speech; to give a light touch and pleasant verisimilitude to a King's proposal of marriage. But verse always keeps the upper hand: few scenes except the obviously comic clown-scenes are entirely in prose.

The style of King Henry's prose is obviously inferior to

that of Prince Hal. It has a certain heaviness which was not present in *Henry IV*. Falstaff spoke better than he knew when he said, "I am not only witty in myself, but the cause that wit is in other men" (*2 Henry IV*, I, ii, 11–12). Hal was brilliant and witty while he had the bulk of Falstaff at which to thrust, and no one spoke better than he when he was attacking Falstaff; Falstaff himself is never better than when he discusses himself ("My lord, I was born about three of the clock in the afternoon . . ."). Hal is not completely unrecognizable in King Henry, but for the most part he speaks like another man. And, in Shakespeare, the speech is always the man.

At this point, before proceeding to examine Shakespeare's most brilliant comic period, we may do well to speak briefly of those plays which have not been considered in any detail, and to review the plays in which his development in the use of prose has been studied.

The first of the two plays whose prose does not greatly concern us is *The Comedy of Errors* (1594); its inconsiderable prose is employed chiefly for the comedy of the two Dromios, which reaches an interesting level in one scene at the most. Other forms—chiefly rhymed verse—usurp the place of prose, and there is only the most elementary type of contrast in this play, whose entire effect depends on the swiftness and singleness of its action.

The second play, *The Merry Wives of Windsor* (1600), is almost wholly in prose, and, for this very fact, is of comparatively slight interest. Shakespeare's reasons for putting the play into prose are not entirely clear; if the legend of Elizabeth's demanding the play of "Falstaff in love" and of Shakespeare's writing it in a fortnight be true, then the prose probably explains itself. Gifted poet though he was, Shakespeare may nevertheless have written prose more rapidly than verse; confronted with a plot and a protagonist which

7*

called for a large measure of prose, he had no reason to hesitate. But this explanation need not rest on a dubious if attractive tradition. Falstaff, however far he may have fallen from his old proud self, is still the indomitable prose speaker of the *Henry IV* cycle; he has lived "to stand at the taunt of one that makes fritters of English," but his prose is yet his own.

What is chiefly important in *The Merry Wives of Windsor* is the reversal of rôles: prose becomes the staple and verse the exception. Verse is reserved for the trifling love-plot and for the rant of Pistol. The play inaugurates an odd and brief period in which Shakespeare will for some reason find prose more congenial and useful than verse. His specific motives are not the same in *The Merry Wives of Windsor*, *As You Like It*, *Twelfth Night* and *Much Ado About Nothing*, but the phenomenon is common to all four plays and merits examination.

A review of the use of prose in the plays discussed would reveal Shakespeare beginning with a mixed heritage: Euphuistic dramatic prose from Lyly, the public domain of clown-prose, and various conventional usages. To this accumulation, he gradually adds original changes and innovations; he extends the province of prose to include non-comic characters such as Shylock; he regularly uses prose to set off his verse and to offer striking contrast to it both in terms of character and of dramatic action. Prose, the form of common speech, introduces an atmosphere of realism; and prose speakers in Shakespeare constantly recall the existence of a world which, although not the "real world" of the audience, is nevertheless somehow physically nearer than the poetic world. His greatest effects of dramatic illusion are obtained by the sense he communicates of the coexistence and interaction of these two worlds. Shakespeare's prose provides a frame and measure for his verse.

8. *As You Like It*

The prose of *As You Like It* (1599), as Rosalind says of
Time, ambles, trots, gallops and—rarely, to be sure—
stands still. It has great variety of movement because virtually every character in the play makes use of it at one time
or another. Prose, both at the court and in the Forest of Ar-
den, is the normal, flexible, and colloquial mode of speech;
verse usually brings an unfamiliar and serious tone into the
otherwise light-hearted play.

The play opens with a prose speech by Orlando, briefly
summarizing his situation. It is one of the shortest and lamest
exposition-scenes in any of the plays; but one is not permitted to dwell on its shortcomings (including the absurdity
of telling Adam what the old man already knows) because
the entrance of Oliver at once brings violent action. Further
exposition is provided, after the brothers' fight, by the conversation of Charles and Oliver.

The second scene opens with the witty prose dialogue of
Rosalind and Celia, which continues with the entrance of
Touchstone. After Orlando's triumph, the Duke asks the
victor his name, and shows his heightened emotional tension
by changing to verse. He leaves at the end of the speech, but
the scene continues in its new tone and in verse to the end.
A similar pattern is followed in the next scene: the cousins
chat together in prose until the Duke and his lords come to
banish Rosalind, after which all speak verse.

In II, iv, Rosalind, Celia, and Touchstone have arrived at
the Forest, and joke in prose about the discomfort of their
journey. Corin and Silvius have a short verse interlude to
discuss the latter's love-pains. Touchstone resumes his
clown's function and breaks into Rosalind's romantic musing
by describing in prose his courting of Jane Smile. Here, in
a single scene, is the play's division of media.

Orlando addresses a formal invocation to the poem which

he pins on a tree (III, ii); the speech consists of two quatrains, alternately rhymed, and a final couplet. If Shakespeare
gives Orlando so elaborate and artificial a form, it is with a
double purpose: an extremely long and witty prose scene
is to follow, providing the maximum contrast in form and
idea to the lover's words and actions; and echoes of Orlando's speech will recur in the poems later found and read
aloud by Rosalind and Celia. Orlando, then, is permitted
to state a theme which will later be parodied in his own mode,
and mocked in the prose which Rosalind will always find
her more natural medium.

Parody and burlesque are not the prerogative of the clown
alone in this play, but they find more direct expression in
Touchstone than in Rosalind. His account of the wooing of
Jane Smile assumes flesh in the courting of Audrey, which is
placed neatly between the beginning of the Orlando-Rosa-
lind romance and the introduction of Silvius and Phebe. For
the latter plot of the swooning lover and cruel charmer,
Shakespeare employs his lushest verse—and unmercifully
mocks it in Rosalind's prose.

Rosalind and Jaques' prose discussion of melancholy, at
the beginning of Act IV, is broken by Orlando's entrance.
His one line of verse, "Good day and happiness, dear Rosalind!" elicits Jaques' sarcastic rejoinder, "Nay then, God
b'wi' you, an you talk in blank verse!" (IV, i, 31-32)—a
further indication of the equation of prose with naturalness.

Silvius interrupts the prose dialogue of Rosalind and
Celia in IV, iii, to discuss in verse the unhappy errand on
which Phebe has sent him. As soon as Rosalind begins to
read the verse letter, she punctuates it with waspish prose
comments, and, at last, breaks out in a prose tirade. The
realism of prose is employed to criticize the lover's foolishness. Oliver's story brings verse for a heightening of tension
which is not dispelled by Rosalind's later jesting in prose.

V, ii, has a formal little verse masque in which Silvius
states a theme and is echoed by the other three lovers. But
Rosalind's ironic participation cannot long amuse her, and
she restores common sense in prose:

> Pray you, no more of this; 'tis like the howling of Irish wolves
> against the moon. (V, ii, 119–120)

The final scene introduces prose, after Rosalind's promise
of a satisfactory conclusion, for Touchstone's extended *jeu
d'esprit* on the punctilio of the quarrel. The revelation of
identity and the short masque are naturally in verse, as are
Jaques de Boys' news and Jaques' general summation. But
Rosalind, as always, has the last word in her prose Epilogue.

Looking back on this play, which rests on a solid base of
prose, one finds a closer balance between verse and prose
than one might expect. There is verse for the scenes of higher
emotional tension, for the idyllic atmosphere of the forest as
dominated by Duke Senior, for Jaques' moralizing and
melancholy reflections, and for the burlesqued pastoral
amours of Phebe and Silvius—but, when the play seeks its
level, it returns inevitably to prose. Rosalind must in large
part be thanked for the dominance of prose, because she is
never really comfortable in verse, a medium quite uncongenial
to her satirical humour. She is the reasonable woman, for all
her weakness, and what she wants to say she can hardly express in verse. She is the woman who is uniquely privileged
in being able to assume an unparalleled objectivity in discussing love with her lover; the quality of that discussion demands prose. Rosalind rules the play and thereby makes
prose supreme. But the rest have discovered the trick without waiting for her lead. Orlando's prose is better than his
verse, although there is little to choose between them. Even
Charles the wrestler can use the form brilliantly:

> They say he is already in the Forest of Arden, and a many merry
> men with him; and there they live like the old Robin Hood of England.

They say many young gentlemen flock to him every day, and fleet the
time carelessly as they did in the golden world. (I, i, 120–125)

Both in the golden world and in the Forest, all can express
themselves in this admirable and facile prose. And the verse,
however good, must doubly justify itself—as it does—to
gain entrance.

The large body of prose is present in the play not merely
because this is a comedy, but because it is a very special sort
of comedy. Rosalind's unique license in the play explains her
oscillation between the poles of romantic love and her realistic, occasionally cynical comic attitude. It must further be
said that Rosalind, even at her most romantic, is never
completely free from skepticism. When she is deeply concerned at Orlando's tardiness at the first meeting of the
course in love, she seems as much amused at her own fits of
passion as she is at Orlando's. Rosalind's great charm lies
in this combination of elements, yet one cannot for a moment doubt the supremacy of the skepticism.

She is not utterly disillusioned like Jaques, to whom she
is opposed; his skepticism has reached the final stage of
self-consuming melancholy. There are definite bounds to
Rosalind's cynicism: no more obvious proof could be asked
than the fact of her marriage to Orlando. Jaques' delight in
melancholy is perverse; Rosalind seeks only a humorous
objectivity which will let her see the world in the only terms
that her healthy and realistic mind will tolerate. This mind
thinks in prose terms; for prose, in Shakespeare, is necessarily the expression of the detached and skeptical intellectual. Rosalind's position in the play permits her to give the
freest possible rein to these qualities. Her disguise puts her
at a remove from all the characters. It is small wonder that,
in this comedy, a detached mind in a detached situation is
given some of Shakespeare's most brilliant comic prose to
speak. *Hamlet* will show the reverse of this coin: the skeptical
mind fettered by circumstances and by itself.

9. *Much Ado About Nothing*

In *As You Like It*, the ascendance of prose arises out of the requirements of the subject-matter and the character of the leading figure, Rosalind. Not even Dover Wilson will suggest that the Rosalind-story was a comic sub-plot in some Ur- *As You Like It;* Lodge's *Rosalynde* is too near Shakespeare's play in time for such fantasy. In *Much Ado About Nothing* (1598–99), however, it is appreciably clear that the older form of the story revolved about Hero and Claudio, and that the introduction of Benedick and Beatrice is Shakespeare's work. Hero and Claudio's plot is the center of almost all the verse in the play; the prose's great bulk (and in no Shakespearean play does the prose so outweigh the verse in every way) tells in purely statistical terms how successfully the comic characters usurp the attention of the dramatist and the action of the play.

The Hero-Claudio love story is introduced at the end of the first scene, which has until then been comic and therefore in prose. Verse reappears briefly in II, iii, in the bantering conversation of Don Pedro, Leonato, Claudio, and Balthasar, after Benedick's long prose monologue. There is skill in this alternation of verse and prose; after Benedick has hidden himself, the newcomers' first lines are spoken loudly, intended for the eavesdropper. Their verse and song do not move him; it is only when the speakers revert to prose and make direct attack that the scoffer is convinced.

In contrast to this scene, with its comic mock-romantic conclusion ("If I do not take pity of her, I am a villain; if I do not love her, I am a Jew. I will go get her picture") (II, iii, 271–273), is the following one, in which Hero and her gentlewomen complete the trick by deceiving Beatrice. Hero speaks her normal verse, and has no difficulty in maintaining a note of high poetic seriousness in her eulogy of Benedick and her account of his love. And Beatrice is so securely trapped that, unlike Benedick, she cannot turn her wit against herself:

> What fire is in mine ears? Can this be true?
>   Stand I condemn'd for pride and scorn so much?
> Contempt, farewell! and maiden pride, adieu!
>   No glory lives behind the back of such.
> And Benedick, love on; I will requite thee,
>   Taming my wild heart to thy loving hand.
> If thou dost love, my kindness shall incite thee,
>   To bind our loves up in a holy band;
> For others say thou dost deserve, and I
> Believe it better than reportingly. (III, i, 107–116)

Shakespeare has to distinguish between two people in the same situation. Benedick simply follows his normal bent, playing his new rôle with gusto while half-mocking himself. Beatrice becomes completely feminine, on the other hand, and relapses not merely into verse but actually into rhymed verse. She becomes as romantic as it is possible for her to be.

The marriage-scene (IV, i) begins in prose but changes to verse at Claudio's interruption. Beatrice and Benedick again speak prose at the end, although their opening lines are serious. The flavor of their earlier prose is missing. They are embarrassed and awkward, words come to them only with difficulty—and small wonder, considering what words they are!—until Beatrice flies into a rage and again becomes perfectly articulate.

The next mixed scene (V, i) begins with the verse dialogue of Leonato and Antonio, and continues in verse after Pedro and Claudio enter. Benedick's entrance causes his friends to change to prose, for they expect to have their customary witty conversation with him. Two prose styles are opposed in their dialogue: the short, angry statements of Benedick and the light, chaffing rejoinders of Pedro and Claudio. Dogberry and Verges introduce their clown-prose after

Benedick's exit, and the revelation of Borachio banishes prose for Claudio and Pedro:

Pedro. Runs not this speech like iron through your blood?
Claudio. I have drunk poison whiles he utter'd it. (V, i, 252–253)

And from this point to the end of the scene only Dogberry and Verges, the clowns, are allowed prose.

The closing scene of the play is in verse up to the revelation of the "no more than reasonable" love of Benedick and Beatrice. With the discovery of the sonnets written in secret by these lovers, surely the most implausible and delightful of all the merry war's absurdities, Benedick calls back prose for the conclusion of the play and must cap even the account of John's arrest with a prose afterword.

The prose of *Much Ado About Nothing* is the lightest, freest, and most natural that Shakespeare ever wrote. Yet it has great variety: Benedick and Beatrice are clearly differentiated in their styles, although they treat much the same matter; the clowns are not to be confused with any others we have known or are to know. The people of this play are most articulate, that is to say, most themselves, in prose.

10. *Twelfth Night*

For all the quantity of prose in *Twelfth Night* (1601), the gross distribution of prose and verse is the familiar one: the sub-plot of Malvolio and his tormentors is regularly in prose, and the chief plot uses verse as a staple, turning to prose for special effects of situation or character. This pattern tends to be constant for most of the comedies; the total picture may on occasion be distorted by the unwontedly large proportion of prose, as in *As You Like It*, where prose-matter and prose characters dominate the principal plot, or as in *Much Ado About Nothing*, where the comic sub-plot displaces the old principal plot, changing the entire character of the play.

In *Twelfth Night*, the only all-prose scenes are those involving some combination of Malvolio, Sir Toby, Sir Andrew, Maria, and Feste. These purely comic scenes (to ignore romantic criticism of Malvolio and his plight) are conventional in technique and are alternated almost regularly with the other scenes.

The mixed scenes are quite another matter. The first, I, v, brings Viola, disguised as a boy, to plead Orsino's suit to Olivia. Viola enters midway in the scene, begins her discourse without ado , and breaks off comically:

> Most radiant, exquisite and unmatchable beauty—I pray you tell me if this be the lady of the house, for I never saw her. I would be loath to cast away my speech; for, besides that it is excellently well penn'd, I have taken great pains to con it. Good beauties, let me sustain no scorn. I am very comptible, even to the least sinister usage.
> (I, v, 181–188)

It requires another fifty-odd lines of prose conversation to convince Viola. Olivia unveils, and Viola, stopping only to wonder whether "God did all," plunges into a praise of her face (in verse, be it noted) and a plea to leave the world a copy. Olivia answers in bantering prose which evokes further and more passionate verse from Viola. Olivia, snared, now speaks verse too, to mark first her growing interest and then her infatuation, until she frankly avows her love in her final soliloquy.

III, i, discovers Viola and Feste conversing in prose. When Viola is left alone, she muses in verse, but returns to prose when Sir Toby and Sir Andrew come in. They are followed by Maria and Olivia, who is at once moved by the sight of Viola, but will speak no verse until the two are left together; they then speak verse throughout the rest of the scene.

The last mixed scene, V, i, begins with comic dialogue

between Orsino and Feste; the prose quickly gives way to verse for a rise in tension at the entrance of Antonio and his captors and reappears only for the speeches of Feste, Sir Toby, and Sir Andrew and the letter of Malvolio.

Twelfth Night does not make extensive use of prose because its principal plot is more sentimental than comic. In this respect it differs markedly from *As You Like It*, where the love-business is fundamentally a serious matter only for Orlando, who therefore uses verse consistently when he knows that he is speaking with Rosalind, or when his emotions overpower him, as in his conversation with the disguised Rosalind. He remains the romantic lover except when the Ganymede-Rosalind can bring him nearer her own mood. But the essential point to note is that Rosalind herself remains free and can consequently indulge her wit and speak prose as freely as she will. She has every power, knowing that her lover is faithful and that she herself is in love. And so the love-plot is developed in comic terms; the romantic aspect requires no development.

The twin elements of plot and character determine the quantity and the nature of the prose in all but Shakespeare's earliest plays. Viola has traits in common with Rosalind, as we discover from her prose, but the situation in which she finds herself does not permit her to give free rein to the expression of these traits. Like Rosalind, she is humorous, witty, and skeptical; Rosalind, however, has every opportunity to display this side of her nature. She is free to give Orlando her considered opinion of the true nature of love—although she may deny her own principles in marrying him—and she can unstintedly enjoy the immunity of her disguise. Viola is not, in this sense, *immune* in her disguise, because she has assumed it to achieve a desired and seemingly hopeless end. She is consequently inhibited and can never fully reveal herself. Rosalind can always retain her objectivity because she never has reason to be uncertain about Orlando. Viola's love remains unrequited until the very dénouement of the play. The two characters are basically different. Rosalind's prose grows out of her humorous and mocking view of the world. She can put aside the romantic element in her nature and speak with the freedom of a man. Viola is a witty, charming, and intelligent woman with no way of expressing her apparently hopeless love. She is fettered by the very disguise which liberates Rosalind. But Viola is in any case made of different stuff; she has not Rosalind's contradictory desire for both freedom and bondage. Her choice is clear; if Rosalind, at the last, seems to agree with her, it is only because the time has not yet come when a Millamant can insist on her provisos.

11. *Measure for Measure*

The most striking use of prose in *Measure for Measure* (1604) is for the Duke's disguise. King Henry V assumed prose with his soldier's cloak to speak, unknown, with his men; but here is a deception which is an integral part of the entire play and which must therefore be maintained much longer and with much greater variety. It is not enough that the Duke deceive a Michael Williams; he must pass unknown before almost all the characters in the play. And, in his assumption of the rôle of a friar, he must seem to exhibit a whole and integrated personality, one whose speech shall have characteristics not known in the Duke's. The Duke, in his disguise, will meet many of the people whom he knows as Duke, but cannot speak with them in his proper person or idiom. As Duke, Vicentio *must* speak verse; as Friar Lodowick, he speaks verse or prose according to the necessities of the situation.

The introductory scene, in which the Duke announces his departure to Escalus and Angelo, is in verse, as befits a formal and solemn delegation of power. The ensuing prose-scene of Lucio and his companions comes as a shock. The entrance of Claudio, midway in the scene, interrupts the prose with a sententious but eloquent verse. This is the Claudio who will later transfigure his own weakness in speaking to Isabella of the universal fear of death. As C. E. Montague has said, "Weak gilded youths like Claudio do not in human experience utter the first masterpieces of human eloquence on any topic. Under the raised arm of death these half-formed characters are more apt to whine and grovel than to state the case for fear so gloriously as almost to give to fear itself a touch of grandeur . . . And yet Claudio's speech sounds ringingly true, because it is a perfect expression not of what any particular man in Claudio's situation was likely to say, from what we know of terrified human nature, but of what we feel to be the most essential thoughts and instincts governing nearly all men so situated, at that time, and expressed by none . . . So, through particular untruth, a universal truth is achieved."[53]

Against Claudio's account of his crime and impending punishment are thrown Lucio's short, cynical prose remarks—and here, as elsewhere in the play, Lucio has something of the satirical commentator about him. He is not a pure specimen of the type, because he enters too much into the action of the play; but the satirical commentator, in his purest form, never appears in Shakespeare as he does in Jonson. All Shakespeare's commentators, Menenius, Thersites, Enobarbus, Apemantus, are made to take a greater part in the action of their plays than do Arruntius or Asper in theirs; and the reason is not far to seek. Shakespeare was too conscientious a craftsman to have much patience with raisonneurs, inactive characters. His one real experiment in this direction—Jaques—is not permitted merely to stand outside the action and criticize it; hardly has he opened his mouth when the

Duke casts aspersions on his motives, his past, and his character. Jaques' satirical speeches are set speeches in the play, without *particular* application to the plot or to any of the characters. He is a mocker and moralizer, but unlike Asper, he points no specific moral. None of Shakespeare's commentators can be said, for example, to be in the situation of Arruntius, in Jonson's *Sejanus*. Arruntius, ostensibly a character in the play, makes such devastating remarks about the progress of the action and the characters of the men involved that his survival must be attributed to a kind of immunity. He must be regarded as having no real part in the play (a construction which Jonson clearly did not put on him) or as being preserved in an almost supernatural way from the fate of Sejanus' other critics. Shakespeare will never permit such questions to arise; he abhors so ambiguous a situation. He is fundamentally no writer of *pièces à thèse*, and it is therefore inconceivable that he should introduce an utterly undramatic commentator whose inspiration and frame of reference lie outside the play.

An indication of how far Lucio departs from the type of the commentator is to be seen in I, iv. He comes to the nunnery to bring Isabella her brother's message, and he speaks to her somewhat roughly, but always in verse. The true commentator would not be drawn into a plot to the extent of bearing messages and falsely defaming a character, as Lucio does the Duke, and he would regularly speak the prose that marks him off from the objects of his criticism.

In III, i, the verse of Claudio and the disguised Duke gives way briefly to prose after Isabella's entrance. The brother and sister, left alone to discuss their moving problem, return at once to verse. When Isabella, revolted, is about to go out, the Duke halts her with a verse line and then, in prose, gives Claudio instructions and reveals to Isabella the story of Mariana and his own plans. The dialogue, from the

Duke's entrance to the end of the scene, is in prose. The Duke's disguise is complete and effective; when he speaks verse, from now on, it is with people who have known him slightly or not at all as Duke; the people who have already been deceived do not suspect him. Thus, in the early part of III, ii, the Duke reproves Pompey in highly moral verse; but, at Lucio's entrance, he first becomes quite taciturn, speaking no more than a dozen words until he is left alone with the newcomer. He then confines himself to short answers in prose, which give him the air of wishing neither to reveal himself nor to pursue the conversation very far. He later expresses his feelings in a verse soliloquy, but returns to prose in the company of others for a sardonic comment on the state of the world: one of the few examples in the comedies of the prose of reduction.

When he is left alone for the last time, he speaks in what is for him an entirely new form, the octosyllabic couplet:

> He who the sword of heaven will bear
> Should be as holy as severe;
> Pattern in himself to know,
> Grace to stand, and virtue go;
> More nor less to others paying
> Than by self-offences weighing... (III, ii, 275 ff.)

The force of this odd speech, coming at the end of a long act in which the Duke has learned the true characters of almost all the people who have surrounded him as Duke, is to summarize in a very pithy and sententious way the results and moral implications of his investigation. The incantation-like quality of the verse (as in *A Midsummer Night's Dream*) emphasizes the quasi-supernatural character of the Duke's rôle: he is the *deus ex machina* transformed into a player of the drama, walking among the rest, set off by an incognito which permits him to observe the malefactors and to engineer their confusion. He is hardly to be accepted as a character on the same level as Angelo or Isabella; he remains always outside the frame of the play and manipulates his puppets with the success of a maladroit playwright.

Except for the Duke's riddling elegy on truth and virtue, all his moral speeches are in verse. In IV, i, he passes from verse to prose within a single speech, moving from a sententious comment on the moral effects of music to matter which more immediately concerns him:

> 'Tis good; though music oft hath such a charm
> To make bad good, and good provoke to harm.

> I pray you tell me, hath anybody enquir'd for me here today?
> Much upon this time have I promis'd here to meet. (IV,i, 14–18)

The conversation of the Provost and Claudio comes as the first verse in IV, ii, in contrast to Pompey's comments on his new profession. Here the change from prose to verse marks the terrible seriousness of Claudio's position, and heightens powerfully the emotional tension of the scene. The extension of this theme in the Duke's talk with the Provost again requires verse. The Messenger's short speech comes as a "prose patch," but by the time the Provost reads the message aloud, he and the Duke have already returned to prose for the practical discussion of immediate tactics.

The single scene of Act V sees only Lucio as a consistent speaker of prose; the Duke, in his own person and in disguise, answers him in prose, but, after the dénouement, Lucio's prose finds no answer. The Duke, once discovered, does not again speak prose; there is no need.

The prose in *Measure for Measure*, barring the comic prose and such conventional usages as Angelo's letter, centers around the Duke's disguise with its attendant complications. It is a remarkable use of prose, and the most extended example of this use in the plays. It provides an additional element of contrast in the play, rendering more complex the construction of individual scenes and elaborating the technical structure of the entire play.

12. *Troilus and Cressida*

Inasmuch as the dominant tone of *Troilus and Cressida* (1602) is satirical, an abundance of prose is to be expected. But in this play it is not only satire that claims prose as its medium; on almost every occasion when prose is used, it has a more or less explicit suggestion of coarseness or cynicism, of skepticism about the values of the world, and of contempt for the people in it.

The most obvious satire is in the direct comments of Thersites. He, of course, speaks only prose; his technique of degradation goes far beyond that of the typical satirical commentator (who is less concerned with gratuitous invective than with moralizing and pointing lessons for his audience in the foolishness he castigates). Thersites follows his victims about, attacks them in public and in private, offers short comments in the form of asides while others are speaking, and, on occasion, summarizes his criticism in monologues.

The first scene of the play at once opposes Troilus, romantic verse and Pandarus' lewd prose. Troilus' love-poetry is in no way unconventional; against his frank avowal and description of his love-melancholy are set Pandarus' cynical comments. These begin on the plane of practical suggestion, pass on to crude remarks about Cressida's beauty, and finally attack Troilus directly in Pandarus' threat to advise Cressida to return to the Greeks. Troilus' passion is contrasted throughout with the cold-blooded cynicism of Pandarus.

The use of prose is one indication that the speaker has some degree of skepticism about the situation in which he finds himself or the characters with whom he shares it. The prose of *Troilus and Cressida* is dedicated almost entirely to mockery. There are, of course, distinguishable degrees: Pandarus' mockery remains on the level of coarse humor which constantly grows more outspoken and more familiar, whereas Thersites speaks always in the bitterest and most unrestrained fashion. Both are cynics, but while Thersites is actually set apart and given some of the privileges of a satirical commentator, Pandarus never seems to be more than a singularly tireless exponent of back-room humor. Thersites, in contrast, is a joyless, humorless mocker. He and Pandarus fulfill similar functions in their respective spheres. Thersites will allow no virtue in the Greek heroes, and Pandarus, through his comments and machinations, finds only lust in the unfortunate amours of Troilus and Cressida. And both cynics impress these ideas on the spectator in their proper language: prose.

The way in which Troilus and Pandarus retain their respective media makes one realize how far Shakespeare has developed since the time when such a situation denoted only the primitive state of the prose-verse play. Jack Cade speaks prose to Lord Say's verse in *2 Henry VI*, and while there is great dramatic effectiveness in this opposition, it is nevertheless the difference in social class which underlies the contrast of media, not, as in the later plays, a subtle distinction of character.

With the breaking-down of the earlier rigid differentiation, there arises, to take its place, no new rule or set of rules, but rather a new and highly flexible principle of creation. The characters and the stuff of the play must determine the choice of medium. Since the possible variations of form are necessarily limited, one cannot be surprised to rediscover patterns that appeared at earlier stages of development. Of these patterns, the consistent opposition of prose to verse by two characters throughout a scene is probably the most interesting. The mixed scene is itself an arresting phenomenon, because it exemplifies in a microcosm the entire complex of problems raised by the prose-verse play. Its divisions are most frequently the causes of the change of form, as in *1 Henry IV*, II, iv, where, after five hundred and fifty lines of prose, verse is used for Hal's conversation with the Sheriff and Carrier. The departure of these worthies is the Prince's cue for the return to prose. Thus the changes of media correspond to some of the dramatic divisions of the scene; within these divisions, either prose or verse is the form used by all the speakers.

When one turns from this type of mixed scene to the type in which various characters regularly speak prose or verse throughout, without regard for the other speakers, the determining feature seems almost always to be character, as in Pandarus' remarks to Troilus, or, indeed, in Pandarus' conversations with any of the verse speakers in the play. These are examples of the most obvious type of contrast; but one must remember that the verse-scene with satirical prose asides also falls within this category. There is no lack of such scenes in Shakespeare's plays: Hamlet's comments during the play-scene offer a notable instance. Essentially, the dramatic significance of this type of mixed scene lies in the *continued* opposition of characters as evidenced by their refusal or inability to change media. Falstaff cannot speak verse; Cloten speaks it briefly (in *Cymbeline*, III, i) but soon reverts to prose, the better to express his clownish nature which cannot accommodate itself even to the gravity of a council of state. The idea of a consistent contrast of forms did not come immediately to Shakespeare; thus, in *Romeo and Juliet*, II, v, the Nurse speaks both prose and verse to Juliet's verse. The consistent contrast between Troilus' verse and Pandarus' prose, with the resulting opposition of character, is a measure of Shakespeare's technical development in the years between *Romeo and Juliet* and *Troilus and Cressida*.

The second scene of the play has a shift from verse to prose which appears to depend only upon a change in tone and in the quality of the subject-matter. Cressida's man tells her in verse of Hector's unwonted rage; when he turns to a description of Ajax, he changes to prose. The shift is anticipated by Cressida's answer to the first statement about Ajax. Hector, even in his fury, is a hero and is so discribed; Ajax, at some unknown best, would still be a lout. Pandarus enters and speaks prose with his niece; he carries his prose like a badge and always justifies his use of it—here in a broad comic vein, and elsewhere in pure bawdiness. After he has left, Cressida normally reverts to verse for the avowal of her love.

Achilles defends Thersites (II, iii) against Patroclus, terming the railer "a privileg'd man," and calls him into his tent to hear him chide further when the Greek lords arrive. If the adjective applied to Thersites has any significance beyond the context of the speech itself, it may underline the commentator's immunity which Thersites in some measure possesses. It might almost be maintained that Shakespeare here tries to justify the presence of an essentially undramatic figure; but, because he will not draw attention to Thersites by marking him out still more, the explanation remains in the form of a single adjective.

The entrance of the lords is recognized in Patroclus' verse answer to Agamemnon; but Ajax, Nestor, and Ulysses speak prose while awaiting Achilles' reply. A contrast is established between the senseless, rambling style of the stupid Ajax and the critical, witty prose of the other two. In the interval of Ulysses' absence, Ajax and Agamemnon unite to praise Ajax in prose, Agamemnon even proposing to send Ajax as an emissary to Achilles. Into the verse of this discussion breaks the prose of satirical asides spoken by Ulysses, Nestor, and even Agamemnon. All three again shift to verse for the final and most fulsome praise of Ajax, which draws him into the plot.

Pandarus and his prose rule the first two scenes of Act III. In the first, Paris and Helen speak prose with him, and verse after his departure. There is a curious conflict in the second scene: Pandarus darts in and out, preparing the encounter, inflaming the already fearful Troilus with short prose speeches. In the intervals of Pandarus' absence from the scene, Troilus speaks verse. At the entrance of Pandarus and Cressida, Troilus has but one line of welcome, for Pandarus, exulting in the proximate consummation of his work, permits himself coarseness and ribaldry in his prose which are unwonted even for him. Troilus and Cressida, alone together, exchange three lines of verse, after which they abruptly and unaccountably change to prose. Various reasons may be suggested: the lovers' unsettled emotional state, or Troilus' attempt to be "witty," following Pandarus' advice. The most plausible explanation lies in the nature of Troilus' speeches: they analyze the bases of love-talk with an objectivity that contrasts oddly with the circumstances. Troilus may be playing for time; Cressida, at all events, has but small taste for this deliberation. She answers him once in his own terms, and then suggests simply, "Will you walk in, my lord?" At Pandarus' final entrance, they assume the verse of lovers and leave prose to him.

In IV, ii, Pandarus' ribald prose jars still more unpleasantly against the lovers' verse; but that verse has no unity of tone. Troilus speaks in the soft phrases and poetic images that the situation demands; but Cressida's language is almost crude, at least as blunt as her reproaches:

> Are you aweary of me?...
> > Prithee tarry.
> You men will never tarry.
> O foolish Cressid! I might have still held off,
> And then you would have tarried. (IV, ii, 7, 15–18)

And her answers to Pandarus are worthy of a daughter of the game. Still, it is only he who speaks prose, for the moment. Aeneas, on entering, addresses him first in verse, but then

mocks him in prose for his quibbling replies. He speaks verse
with Troilus. Later in the scene, Cressida's prose reflects her
anxiety and confusion; when she learns the news, she rises
to the occasion with two high-flown verse speeches.

Thersites and Ulysses bait Troilus in V, ii, while the latter watches Cressida and Diomed, Thersites railing in prose,
Ulysses alternately persuading Troilus to silence and playing
the *faux ingénu* in verse. Thersites is left alone on the stage
at the end of the scene, as at the end of V, i, to remind the
audience that only wars and lechery hold fashion. The rest
of the play's prose, except for the first part of Pandarus' final admonition to the panders of the audience, is Thersites'.
Thersites has beyond question a primarily satirical function
in the play. His prose systematically vulgarizes the heroes
and reduces their dimensions. But satire, and particularly
Elizabethan satire, is rarely pointless; it has at least a pur-
gative function, which sometimes may damage or diminish
the artistic excellence of its literary medium, as in Jonson's
Every Man Out of His Humour.[54] The satirized characters
are either obliged to confess the stupidity of their humours,
or forced to reveal their utter confusion. But nothing of the
sort happens to Thersites' victims, nor does he himself seem
to have any specific purpose in holding them up to scorn. In
his last appearances, he generalizes from his observations, but
appears to find little pleasure in his conclusions. A kind of disinterested misanthropy seems to drive him through the play.

The prose in *Troilus and Cressida* is almost entirely the
property of two characters: the railer and the bawd. The first
vilifies the heroes, the second the lovers of the play.

13. *The Winter's Tale*

The Winter's Tale (1611) opens with an exposition-scene
in prose. Like most examples of the type, this scene employs
two characters who tell each other what both already know.

The two men, Camillo and Archidamus, are lords; their conversation is in a light, courtly prose. Since the following scene of the two Kings and the Queen is to continue, with elaborations and unexpected changes, the themes announced in the first scene, a nice contrast is set up between the casualness of the introductory scene and the passion of the second.

The indictment of Hermione and the message of the Delphic oracle (II, ii), both perfect examples of conventional prose, have a special force in their contexts. The dry, matter-of-fact indictment is followed by Hermione's passionate verse self-defense. And the confusion of the trial-scene is pierced through by the short, bald phrases of the oracle:

> 'Hermione is chaste; Polixenes blameless; Camillo a true subject; Leontes a jealous tyrant; his innocent babe truly begotten; and the king shall live without an heir if that which is lost be not found.' (III, ii, 132–136)

At the end of Act III comes the most unexpected and delightful prose of the play. Antigonus' horrific exit, "pursued by a bear," leaves Perdita alone on the shore. To her come the Shepherd, humorously berating the local youths for driving off his sheep, and the Clown, bursting with his news of the tragedies on land and sea. The distortion of these violent actions in the Clown's description provides us finally with the transition from the melodrama of the first three acts to the pastoral beauty of the fourth and the recognition and reconciliation of the fifth.

From this point on, prose begins to play a more significant part in the action. Autolycus, the play's greatest prose speaker, appears in IV, iii, describing himself in unforgettable terms. In scene iv, he and his gulls create an admirable prose interlude between Perdita's flower-scene and the lovers' discovery by Polixenes. When, later, Camillo and Florizel invite Autolycus to join in their plot, they speak prose with him; in their private discussions, the two nobles use verse.

The last prose scene (V, ii) is another exposition-scene in which Autolycus solicits information which the anonymous Gentleman is only too ready to give. A second Gentleman and then a third appear, each bringing more news. Shakespeare, both by using Autolycus and by bringing on so many speakers, seems to make a fairly determined attempt to render his exposition dramatically plausible.

Prose is not used extensively in *The Winter's Tale;* it finds its place in exposition-scenes, clown-interludes, and other conventional devices. It is, however, very beautifully written. Autolycus is a comic character built up entirely in prose, the best and most complete after Falstaff. But the nature of the play forces him into a subordinate part. The use of prose in exposition-scenes suggests Shakespeare's desire to render his exposition more natural by introducing it into casual conversation, and by employing characters who actually have some interest in the events described.

14. *Cymbeline*

Prose does not appear in *Cymbeline* (?1610) until the second scene of the first act, in the dialogue of the absurd Cloten and the two Lords. The delay is significant. The first scene has set the stage for the play's high passions and frankly melodramatic situation. The entrance of the vainglorious Cloten, whom Imogen has defamed, and whose every remark is burlesqued in an aside by the Second Lord, comes as a shock and a disappointment. Cloten's prose emphasizes his clownish qualities; he is not to be taken seriously, and all that he says is at once reduced to laughter by the mocking echo. But the scene is not merely a clown's interlude, for it develops the last incident introduced into the plot at the end of the first scene, and also affords a contrast between the violence of that scene and the tenderness of the following one.

The contrast is maintained in the fourth scene, in which Iachimo and Posthumus meet and arrange their incredible wager. Against the verse in which Imogen has told Pisanio of her love for Posthumus stand Iachimo's prose of degradation and the curt, unwilling responses of Posthumus.

It is true that Cloten's "normal" form of speech is prose, but his use of that medium is clearly governed by the dramatic situation. Thus, in II, iii, he first speaks prose, in the character of a clown, and then verse, as the ridiculous lover. Similarly, in III, i, Cloten makes his first martial speech in verse, but his later clownish interruptions in prose.

Prose letters appear in two verse scenes, III, ii and iv. They are Posthumus' dissembling letter to Imogen, which draws her to Milford Haven, and his order to Pisanio for the murder of Imogen. The first letter is surrounded by verse the simplicity and directness of which make the prose sound stilted; the prose of the second letter is so passionate and simple that Pisanio's verse comment seems unnecessarily elaborate and flowery. In contrast, Imogen's own verse is almost unbearably direct. For a great part of the play, Imogen and Posthumus speak together only in such interchanges, so that, while Imogen appears as the incarnation of honesty and fidelity, one is aware of Posthumus either behind the mask of formal phrases or as an incredibly gullible and cruel dupe. He speaks to Imogen through these prose letters, and does nothing to alter the impression of stupidity and insensitivity which he has given the audience in making the wager with Iachimo. No prose could well compete with Imogen's verse in any case; that of Posthumus must surely fail.

Cloten speaks verse in III, v, until he tries to buy Pisanio as an ally, and changes to prose. His speech becomes ever more unsettled; he darts from one idea to another, jumbling his thoughts and expression. Prose, as always, mirrors this confusion more faithfully than verse. Cloten's character as clown reappears briefly in IV, i, where he again tells his plans for Imogen and Posthumus. He can use even so typically clownish a device as the pun:

How fit his garments serve me! Why should his mistress, who was made by him that made the tailor, not be fit too? the rather (saving reverence of the word) for 'tis said a woman's fitness comes by fits. (IV, i, 2–7)

But he is accorded verse for his death, perhaps more to save the dignity of the scene than his own.

Posthumus' scene in prison (V, iv) employs a variety of forms. He himself begins with a soliloquy in blank verse; then, while he is asleep, the ghosts perform a masque, speaking irregular stanzas with short and even unrhymed lines. Jupiter interrupts their prayers with a long speech in iambic pentameter quatrains. Sicilius' last lines are in normal blank verse, ending with a couplet. The short, formal lines of the masque contribute to the sense of unreality it creates. Posthumus awakes to find the prophecy, which, obeying the convention, is in prose. The Jailer's entrance brings a prose dialogue of notable excellence. The Jailer's prose is very fine; its periods are short, its vocabulary clipped and pungent. It is, in a sense, a *tour de force*, because its possible dramatic function of relaxation has been rendered superfluous by the revelations of the masque. Posthumus is in no real danger, and the audience does not require relief before violent action recommences. The episode serves, however, as a transition scene between the masque, with its promise of reconciliation, and the dénouement. It recalls the perils which are past (incidentally introducing a brilliant natural philosopher) and enables one to face with equanimity the innumerable recognitions, discoveries, and reconciliations of the final scene.

Cymbeline's prose helps to delineate Cloten as a kind of

clown and to mark him off from the rest of the court; it gives fine dramatic point to the play's letters; and, as always, it contributes to the portrayal of character and maintains a dramatic opposition to verse.

15. *The Tempest*

The greatest part of the prose in *The Tempest* (1611) belongs to Stephano and Trinculo, since they, more than anyone else, are the play's clowns. In this respect, it is interesting to see that Caliban speaks almost only verse, even with the drunken servants. For Caliban is no clown, whatever else he may be. He is a savage and a primitive, with a dignity in his nature that is totally absent in Stephano and Trinculo. Caliban is warped and evil, but at his lowest he retains qualities that make him a worthier opponent for Prospero than the two petty rogues could ever be.

The play opens with prose: the stage is full of sailors, shouting and running about confusedly, the Boatswain calling out his orders rapidly and pushing the helpless courtiers out of the way. The latter are too bewildered and frightened to speak anything more rigidly connected than prose. They have time, of course, to curse the rude Boatswain, and their curses are hardly noble or dignified enough for verse. Gonzalo's comic speeches at once establish him as a dry and humorous character and relieve the tension. The mounting sense of hopelessness is conveyed by the shift from prose to verse at the entrance of the mariners, summoning the rest to prayers. But, at the end of the scene, Gonzalo is left alone and speaks a few lines of comic prose. Thus it is hinted that the danger is somehow unreal, and that the expectation of disaster has been created only to be disappointed. After "Let's all sink with th' King," and "Let's take leave of him," the air is cleared by "I would fain die a dry death."

Gonzalo begins II, i, by attempting to comfort Alonso. The old man's sententious condolences evoke irritation in Alonso and mockery in Antonio and Sebastian, who openly jeer at him in prose. He at first tries to continue in verse in spite of them, but soon undertakes to defend himself, speaking prose like them. Alonso's verse outburst recalls the three to themselves and to verse. Prose returns for another comic passage after Gonzalo's paraphrase of Montaigne.

Caliban's first speeches to Trinculo in II, ii, are frightened, breathless ejaculations; he speaks prose because his words are forced from him by fear: "Do not torment me! O!" and "The spirit torments me. O!" Reassured, if momentarily, he returns to his normal verse:

> Thou dost me yet but little hurt.
> Thou wilt anon; I know it by thy trembling.
> Now Prosper works upon thee. (II, ii, 82–84)

By the time Caliban speaks again, the "celestial liquor" has quite won him over, and he continues in verse. He twice drops into prose, swearing his fealty to his new master. In his lyrical speeches, which again reveal him as the primitive whose knowledge and thought are expressed entirely in terms of the island world, he uses verse. His final speech is a mixture of drunken song and prose. The sober Caliban is always a verse speaker, however, as is seen in III, ii, when he incites his confederates to fall upon Prospero and kill him: a curious scene, which seems to look forward to an unrealized development of the plot. Stephano and Trinculo regularly answer Caliban in prose, but Caliban retains his verse and at last rises to a great lyric height in his account of the island's enchantments.

Prose is used in *The Tempest* for comic or semi-comic scenes, and to suggest that apparently imminent tragedy will be averted. Caliban's very sparing use of prose is noteworthy as marking him off from his companions. Prose plays so small a part in *The Tempest* because the prose speakers in the play themselves count for so little. Lines of action for the sub-plot of the clowns' conspiracy against Prospero are laid down by Caliban's repeated warnings that the books must be burnt; but all this comes to nothing.

Shakespeare's use of prose in his comedies becomes most extensive at the middle of his career and thereafter shows a fairly steady decline. Prose is more and more restricted to specific characters and elements in the plot. The ratio of prose to verse remains substantial, but grows perceptibly smaller.

The dramatic value of prose certainly does not diminish. The nature of Shakespearean comedy has been altered and no longer requires so great a quantity of prose as Shakespeare used in his middle period. The tragedies, although displaying a similar decline in quantity of prose, continue to use prose freely and richly for dramatic effect. Rylands' suggestion that Shakespeare, in his later plays, succeeded in making his verse do all the work of prose seems implausible. Were this true, it would be difficult to understand why Shakespeare did not altogether dispense with prose in those plays. He appears, on the contrary, to have felt that prose still played a vital part in the dramatic structure of his work.

V

Shakespeare: The Tragedies

Comedy finds in prose a highly appropriate medium; tragedy and chronicle history, on the other hand, seem to exhibit no obvious need for prose, and the three plays by Shakespeare in which no prose appears are all chronicle histories on tragic themes: *King John, 3 Henry VI,* and *Richard II.* But the fact is that prose is quite as essential to Shakespearean tragedy as to Shakespearean comedy; basically dramatic function of prose in Shakespeare's the work shows itself even more clearly in the non-comic plays than in the comedies. In comedy, the contrasting elements are likely to be widely separated within the play. As many characters, rather than few, tend to speak prose, the use of prose for delineation of character or for dramatic contrast becomes more subtle, because the oppositions of form are less violent. Levels of comedy may be opposed, comic action differentiated from romantic intrigue or melodrama, and satirical commentators set apart from their prey. But as even the most violent passions are, in comedy, eventually frustrated or resolved, they become, as it were, potentially susceptible of being treated in prose.

It is never so with tragedy. The opposing quantities remain constant. When they seem to approach each other, it is only in order that the contrast may ultimately be heightened.

It has been suggested by Mr. C. L. Barber that prose in Shakespeare's tragedies is an extended use of comic prose analogous to the use of prose in the comedies themselves. Granted that striking parallels can be traced between Lear's mad prose and typical clown-prose, the vital question of *purpose* remains: does Lear speak clown-prose for the reasons of a Launce or of a Falstaff? The element of comic relaxation is certainly not present in Lear's prose; the kind of contrast afforded by Launce is totally unlike the verse-prose opposition in the speech of Lear, whose verse helps to depict a choleric old man, but whose prose portrays a disintegrating mind. In *King Lear*, III, vi, the context of the Fool's lines robs them of any possible comic effect; Lear seizes on the Fool's question and relates it to his own situation. A little later in the same scene, the distinction between prose and verse breaks down almost entirely; the result is harmony, not contrast. The comic element of the Fool's prose is assimilated to the overwhelmingly tragic intent of the scene. Thus *King Lear* employs the forms, but not the spirit, of comedy.

Because prose enters more normally into comedy than into tragedy, a certain conservatism in Shakespeare's extension of the uses of prose in his earlier histories and tragedies can be marked. His generous employment of prose in his earliest comedies obliged him from the first to begin developing and elaborating his comic prose. His first tragedies, which used prose sparingly or not at all, obviously made no such demands on his resources. From *Romeo and Juliet* onward, however, this lag disappears, and a *Hamlet* or an *Othello* shows how richly the prose-verse play could deal with tragic material. Prose in *2 Henry VI* or in *Richard III* is an intrusion, however skillfully effected; prose in *Romeo and Juliet* and in virtually every tragedy thereafter is an integral part of the play.

1. *2 Henry VI*

The unique appearance of prose in *1 Henry VI*—the reading of the riot act in I, iii—may pass without comment.

9

The rigidity of the old convention of prose for documents and proclamations may be judged from the fact that Shakespeare found it necessary to insert these eight lines of prose into a play which is otherwise entirely in verse. It cannot be denied that the prose successfully creates, in the midst of the violence, an atmosphere which might be styled *legal*; it produces the desired effect of stifling action.

Another prose document is brought into the action in the first scene of *2 Henry VI* (?1590–91). Gloucester seems to be intended to stumble in reading the peace treaty aloud; his actual dropping of the paper is the final outward expression of his dismay and anger. The bald and flat prose stands in startling opposition to the passion it provokes, both in Gloucester's immediate action and in his later speech. The reading of the treaty appears as a prose interruption in the midst of a verse scene.

The petitioners enter in I, iii, and with them comes the play's basic prose element. Here, at least, one can for once agree with the rather primitive view that Shakespeare uses prose to separate the lower classes from the aristocracy. But prose is not the fundamental element differentiating the petitioners from the Queen and Suffolk, for Suffolk himself speaks prose in addressing them, prose as haughty and contemptuous as any verse. The plebeians are servile and fearful, and their prose consorts well with their lack of dignity. Suffolk's use of prose expresses, all the same, a kind of condescension, for the Queen will deign only to drive out the men with four lines of verse. When Peter and his master are brought back, later in the scene, to be tried in the King's presence, they alone speak prose.

The explanation of the prose with which scene iv opens is less clear: the conjurers Hume and Bolingbroke may speak prose because they belong to a class lower than that of Eleanor; it would then be necessary to find some other explana-

tion for Bolingbroke's verse speech which prepares the beginning of the conjuring. A more plausible and consistent
interpretation would show the first speeches as setting the
stage for the Duchess' entrance and summing up, in a brief
and even awkward bit of exposition, the background of the
present situation. The Duchess herself is impatient for the
rites to begin, and, in prose, admonishes the conjurers, who
are after all her servants. Bolingbroke's professional pride
is irked by this scant courtesy, and he therefore answers her
with dignity in verse.

The Simpcox episode (II, i) involves a curious confusion
of forms, which appears to have no underlying significance.
The first part of the episode employs verse for the King and
nobles, and either broken verse or prose for Simpcox, his
wife, and the townsfolk. The dialogue of the cross-examina-
tion is printed as verse, but it is irregular and the total effect
is surely that of prose. For example:

> *Cardinal.* What, art thou lame?
> *Simpcox.*   Ay, God Almighty help me!
> *Suffolk.* How cam'st thou so?
> *Simpcox.*   A fall off of a tree.
> *Wife.* A plum tree, master. (II, i, 95–97)

At the end of the scene, Gloucester abandons both his verse
and the condescending, mocking prose of his short answers,
and berates Simpcox in straightforward, well-knit argumenta-
tive prose. He gathers the strands of the snares he has been
preparing for the poor knave, brings the scene to its dénouement, and prepares the complete physical rout of the whip-
ping. With the exit of the Simpcoxes, the scene at once reverts to verse.

The Simpcox story stands as a comic interlude within
the scene. Shakespeare's incomplete solution of the question
of form is related to the whole problem of the interpolated
comic scene in the earlier Elizabethan drama. For prose has

9*

not yet been firmly established as the sole form for comedy and comic scenes. Doggerel, as preserved in the jigs, remains a powerful competitor, and doggerel elements are still to be seen in the episode just examined, together with a kind of crude stichomythia. These verse elements point to a certain formalism in at least the earlier part of the scene, which the fabulous and folk-tale quality of the incident may help to explain. Prose becomes dominant at the end because of Gloucester's *raisonnement;* it explains and resolves the action and writes as full a stop after it as a couplet can supply.

Another interpolated prose scene (II, iii) is the trial by combat of Peter and the Armourer, which follows on the far more tragic condemnation of the Duchess of Gloucester. The entire scene thus deals with the dispensation of justice, first by the King and then by the intervention of God. The Duchess' banishment is promptly followed by the Duke's fall from power; into this tense atmosphere come Horner and Peter, each surrounded by a group of cheerful and drunken supporters, who effectively banish solemnity and dignity from the stage. So well is a vulgar and comic mood established that Horner's death comes as something of a shock. Peter's delirious self-recognition as the instrument of God is echoed by Henry's pompous verse speech.

The rest of the prose in the play is connected with the rebellion of Jack Cade, and may therefore be considered comic prose to the same degree that the entire Cade sequence is comic. The arrangement of the units of this sequence is interesting: first comes the exposition-scene of Bevis and Holland; then Cade's account of his noble birth (with the ironical comments of Butcher and Smith); the condemnation and execution of the Clerk; and finally the Stafford episode. In his encounter with Sir Humphrey Stafford, Cade, *alias* Sir John Mortimer, addresses Sir Humphrey in the verse which he takes to be the proper form for one of his rank.

Cade's final contemptuous speeches of dismissal are again in prose, however, for they are addressed to his followers as much as to Sir Humphrey. Cade allows himself one pseudo-heroic verse speech to his men after the Staffords' departure; he speaks in his character as Mortimer and now, too, as the leader of an army. In the next scene (IV, iii) Cade returns to prose once more to exchange a few comments with Butcher.

Cade's verse is but another mark of his presumption, for, in the two scenes remaining to him, he speaks only prose, opposed in each case by a verse speaker. In IV, vii, Cade's scurrilous and incoherent prose is pitted against the noble and simple verse of Lord Say; and perhaps nothing isolates Say in the rebel camp so much as his use of verse. Here the less significant determinant of form, social class, unites with the element of differentiation of character to produce a mixed scene not unworthy of a more mature play.

Similarly, the scene of Cade's death (IV, x) offers Cade a verse-speaking opponent in Alexander Iden, the Kentish squire. Iden is presented as the homely embodiment and exponent of the national virtues, and it is as such that he fights and kills the rebel Cade. Iden's use of verse ennobles him as much as does the matter of his smug little speech.

The characters in *2 Henry VI* admittedly speak prose or verse according to their social rank. The conflict of the upper and lower classes is expressed both in action and in the opposition of their forms of speech. *2 Henry VI* shows Shakespeare's dramatic prose in its most primitive stage, but already being used for contrast with verse.

2. *Titus Andronicus*

This dreary product of Shakespeare's novitiate in tragedy, probably written in 1593, has no more than thirty lines in prose, which would be without interest did they not show an early version of a familiar Shakespearean device. In the passage in question, toward the end of IV, iii, a Clown comes to Titus and Marcus, who take him for a messenger and command him to bear Titus' supplication to Saturnine. He unwillingly assents.

The conversation between the Andronici and the Clown is in prose, until the latter makes a punning answer to Titus' first request that he represent them before the Emperor. Titus then addresses the Clown curtly in verse, and repeats his first question, in altered form, in prose:

> Sirrah, come hither. Make no more ado,
> But give your pigeons to the Emperor,
> By me thou shalt have justice at his hands.
> Hold, hold!. Meanwhile here's money for thy charges.
> Give me pen and ink, Sirrah, can you with a grace deliver a suppli-
> cation? (IV, iii, 102–107)

The Clown naturally does not refuse a second time. Titus again speaks to him in prose, after which he turns and addresses his brother in verse. In the following scene the Clown speaks a few prose lines to Saturnine before the order is given for his hanging.

The way is prepared for the introduction of comic matter by Titus' distracted ravings. Shakespeare has not yet arrived at that stage of his development where the madness of a tragic hero expresses itself in the prose of a Lear. Ercles' vein is sufficient for Titus, and yet he is capable of a certain grim humor when he takes the Clown for a messenger from Jupiter, thereby establishing a comic atmosphere for the ensuing dialogue.

There is little profundity of dramatic art in having Titus change from prose to verse, to mark his irritation with the Clown, but Shakespeare's use of this device in so primitive a play is nevertheless notable. The subtler developments of this and other devices will follow; it is enough that they already exist in germ. The Clown is introduced when Titus has gone mad, or nearly so; the juxtaposition of comedy and madness in *Titus Andronicus* and in *King Lear* is the only element common to the two plays, but it is a significant one. The psychological association is to undergo great deepening and elaboration. But the impulse and conception which will adorn Shakespeare's most mature play already show themselves in his least mature.

3. *Richard III*

Limited use of prose in a play may be as revealing as more extended use. When, as in *Richard III* (?1592), prose is found only in a part of one scene, one wonders why it is there at all; even in so relatively mature a play as *King John*, Shakespeare was able to dispense entirely with prose. He did so not by eliminating scenes that one might expect to find in prose, but by casting such scenes in verse. To include, therefore, seventy lines of prose in a play which is otherwise in verse, seems in many ways curious, and one feels Shakespeare could neither delete the scene nor treat it in verse.

The episode in question is the murder of Clarence (I, iv). The two murderers present their warrant to Brakenbury, who deliberately refuses to understand their mission in order to absolve himself of responsibility. The Second Murderer is now conscience-stricken at the thought of murdering Clarence, and argues with his companion. This discussion, which affords so odd a digression at a moment when violent action is expected, accomplishes two ends: it protracts the suspense, by disappointing the audience's expectation, only to fulfill it after all; and it increases one's sense of the horror of the deed by showing that even the instruments of murder are affected by it.

In their few speeches, the two murderers to some extent

reveal their characters. The First Murderer is a fairly callous tool, although he can say of his conscience: "It is even now at my elbow, persuading me not to kill the Duke." (I, iv, 149-150). And he is suspiciously eager to drop the whole affair, to return to Richard, and to inform him of the Second Murderer's hesitation. The latter's courage is screwed not quite to the sticking-point; he wants to get the dirty business done quickly, or to shirk it, and he vacillates between these alternatives. He flees after the killing, leaving the First Murderer to collect the entire fee.

The quality of this dialogue, in itself, is comic; the context, however, so completely overshadows the comic element that the situation is more dreadful than it would be without this interruption. The monologue of the Porter in *Macbeth* comes after the murder of Duncan, and the Porter himself has not been involved; here, the murderers themselves engage in a semi-humorous colloquy dealing with the murder they are to commit. The Second Murderer's joking seems at times almost hysterical; he seizes on a theme and embroiders it in such a way that one can only think him to be playing for time:

1. Murd. So, when [Richard] opens his purse to give us our reward, thy conscience flies out.

2. Murd. 'Tis no matter; let it go. There's few or none will entertain it.

1. Murd. What if it come to thee again?

2. Murd. I'll not meddle with it; it makes a man a coward. A man cannot steal, but it accuseth him; a man cannot swear, but it checks him; a man cannot lie with his neighbour's wife, but it detects him. 'Tis a blushing shamefac'd spirit that mutinies in a man's bosom. It fills a man full of obstacles. It made me once restore a purse of gold that (by chance) I found. It beggars any man that keeps it. It is turn'd out of towns and cities for a dangerous thing, and every man that means to live well endeavours to trust to himself and live without it. (I, iv, 132–148)

Several reasons, then, seem to have moved Shakespeare to

cast these few lines of *Richard III* in prose. The Murderers are of low degree (Clarence tells the First Murderer, "Thy voice is thunder, but thy looks are humble"); they hesitate, and therefore discuss the ethics of murder and the necessity for disregarding their consciences, thereby intensifying the suspense and terror of the situation. Prose is used to characterize the Murderers and to contrast them with their victim. Moreover, the prevailing grotesquely comic and satirical tone of their dialogue dictates the use of prose.

4. *Romeo and Juliet*

Romeo and Juliet (?1595) is Shakespeare's first great achievement in the mixed form. For the poetry and prose of this play complement each other exquisitely. Some of the prose ranks with the most pleasing in all the plays; it is light and gracefully turned, Shakespeare's most brilliant badinage before *As You Like It*, and it so successfully contributes to the achievement of dramatic effect that *Romeo and Juliet* is the first play in which prose and verse are put on the same level and made to enhance each other on terms of absolute parity. Not all the prose sparkles as Mercutio's does; but then not all the prose speakers are Mercutios. Shakespeare had long since given evidence of his high artistry in the writing of prose; but he had not previously made the journeyman clown-prose of Sampson and Gregory serve larger dramatic ends.

The play opens with this conversation of the two Capulet servants, who joke about their valiance and belligerence. Their dialogue and their quarrel with Abram and Balthasar (which the braggart Sampson so unwillingly provokes) is at once a burlesque of their masters' feud and a presage of tragic events to come.

This prose gambit is artful in the extreme. The tragedy begins with a comic degradation of the senseless family feud, presented in low and vulgar terms. Gregory precipitates the scuffle with the Montagues' men only when he spies Benvolio and becomes eager to make a good showing before one of his masters. The advent of Tybalt touches off the more serious conflict.

The scene opens in a low key in prose, rising with the Tybalt-Benvolio fight and the entrance of Old Capulet and Old Montague to the high point of the Prince's verse speech. Thus the entire dramatic presentation of the feud is set in a completely realistic frame. One is prepared from the start to find the feud insane; the clowns reduce it to absurdity. There is a deadly parallel between their brawling and the aristocratic swashbuckling of a Tybalt.

An otherwise undistinguished clown passage (I, ii) gains ironic force from the fact that the Clown serves as unconscious intermediary between Old Capulet and Romeo and thus becomes the agent of the meeting of Romeo and Juliet. The Clown is commanded to deliver the invitations to guests whose names he cannot read, and therefore seeks help of Romeo, who takes the opportunity to make ironic quibbles on the Clown's words. This exchange is perfectly conventional: Romeo and Benvolio do not cease to speak verse, although they are addressed in prose. The servingman who brings I, iii, to a conclusion also speaks prose, but in his capacity as clown rather than as servant:

> Madam, the guests are come, supper serv'd up, you call'd, my young lady ask'd for, the nurse curs'd in the pantry, and everything in extremity. I must hence to wait. I beseech you follow straight (I, iii, 100-104)

Surely these are the rhythms of Launce.

Clownish servingmen also open the scene of the Capulets' feast. Their prose dialogue communicates realistically a sense of the backstairs life in a great house such as the Capulets'. While the aristocrats play their amorous games,

Susan Grindstone and Nell slip past the porter to the servants' hall. The object of the comic gambit is, however, only
incidentally ironic; it is, above all, intended to suggest the
bustle and confusion of a great social gathering, the lightness
and gaiety against which Romeo's new-born love shows
itself, and which it must transcend to prove itself sincere. The
scene moves from comedy through the avowal of love to end
on a note of tragic foreboding.

Romeo appears in II, iv, in the character of a gallant and
wit whom Mercutio (on the basis of what must be regarded as insufficient evidence) owns his superior. Their
prose wit-combat offers some idea of the "real" Romeo, a
man who never appears in the play, for he is seen first in love
with Rosaline and then with Juliet. The brilliance of the
quibbling dialogue must be taken on faith; that Mercutio's
spirit, as well as his wit, begins to flag, may be gathered
from the enthusiasm he shows in attacking the Nurse.

The excellence of this scene consists in its portrayal of
Mercutio; his prose is a constant delight, ever in motion,
shifting its ground, suddenly parrying and thrusting. He
is what he suggests that Romeo was before being stabbed
with a white wench's black eye. But Romeo is not long permitted to play this part. Mercutio sings his song and departs,
taking Benvolio with him; Romeo can now receive his message. Although he has until now spoken prose, he changes to
verse to give the Nurse directions for Juliet. The Nurse herself is sufficiently moved by the seriousness of the discussion
to forego prose, although she eventually relapses and babbles
her last speeches in prose.

This scene and the following one, in which the plans for
the elopement are made, move swiftly and lightly to the marriage that concludes the act. The comic dialogue of Romeo
and Mercutio, with its suggestions of the earlier Romeo, provides a contrast to the otherwise unvaried portrait of the

lover. The Nurse will not cease her flow of language to hear orders from Romeo, just as she will not leave off complaining to give those orders to Juliet. But the interruptions caused by her senseless chat only intensify the speed of the action.

Mercutio's prose reaches its high point in III, i, but it is a swan song. He begins by indulging in pleasant fooling with Benvolio, pretending to take the latter for a hot-headed swordsman. The description may not fit Benvolio, but it is the portrait of Tybalt, who addresses the two men provocatively and finds Mercutio more than ready for him. Mercutio's anger causes him to leave his bandying prose for a coldly insulting verse. The entrance of Romeo draws Tybalt's attention. Romeo's refusal to fight arouses Mercutio, whose challenge is given and accepted in verse. Mercutio's first words after receiving his death wound are in verse, but he rallies to speak his own obituary in prose of his best style:

> No, t'is not so deep as a well, nor so wide as a church door; but 'tis enough, 'twill serve. Ask for me to-morrow, and you shall find me a grave man. I am peppered, I warrant, for this world. A plague o' both your houses! Zounds, a dog, a rat, a mouse, a cat, to scratch a man to death! A braggart, a rogue, a villain, that fights by the book of arithmetic! Why the devil came you between us? I was hurt under your arm. (III, i, 99–108)

For his last lines, however, he returns to verse; Shakespeare gives him the dignity of verse for his death. Romeo has nothing to say but that most ineffectual of all lines, "I thought all for the best."

With Mercutio's death, the play loses all lightness. Its swiftness becomes a headlong rush to the inevitable catastrophe. Mercutio has served as a link between the matter of the play and Romeo's previous history; his witty and cynical mind has afforded an effective foil for his fellow, now turned lover. His unnecessary death begins the series of tragedies that can end only in the destruction of Romeo and Juliet.

It seems hardly possible that the play, after the death of its most brilliant prose speaker and the tragic events following, should yet find use for a comic prose scene. The presence of such a scene therefore indicates Shakespeare's desire to achieve some special effect—or to satisfy Will Kempe's demand for a longer part, as the casualness of this comic matter may indicate. The Nurse discovers Juliet, apparently dead (IV, v) and assembles a large company with her screams. All eventually leave except the Musicians, to whom comes Peter the clown with a request to play; he remains to joke with them in a prose dialogue half as long again as the tragic scene immediately preceding. The mixture of tragedy and low comedy would be unbearable if the mourning were not without reason.

Romeo and Juliet is the first of Shakespeare's tragedies in which prose plays an important part. The comic prose sets the scene for serious action, as in the first scene, or nullifies the effect of tragic events, as in IV, v. The character of Mercutio is built up in witty, courtly prose, and, through him, the atmosphere of young gallantry in Verona. At all times, the interplay of prose and verse is strongly marked. This most lyrical of Shakespeare's plays owes much of its dramatic effectiveness to its prose.

5. *Julius Cæsar*

Julius Cæsar (1599), like *Romeo and Juliet,* begins with a short prose episode which frames the action of the play. Flavius and Marullus, the Tribunes, are discovered driving some workingmen to their homes. The Cobbler, a self-appointed spokesman, explains, after quibbling and equivocating with his questioners, that he and his fellows have left their work to celebrate Cæsar's triumphant return to Rome. The Tribunes then recall Pompey's greatness and reproach the mob for its fickleness. Their verse, noble and lofty in its anger, easily beats down the Cobbler's clown prose.

It is an admirable opening scene in its foreshadowing of two great themes of the play: the nobility and sincerity of Cæsar's opponents, and the fickleness of the mob. The plebs loved Pompey; they now adore Cæsar; they will twice again change masters. The clown prose, moreover, has special weight in this scene. The Cobbler speaks prose because he is not merely a "mechanical," but also witless. He has gone forth from his shop to cheer one hero; formerly he cheered that hero's enemy. In his senseless joking with the Tribunes, he is revealed as a totally irrational man. And Brutus will precipitate his own tragedy by his determination to deal with the Cobbler as though the latter were a completely rational man.

After Cæsar's exit, in I, ii, Brutus and Cassius induce Casca to describe for them the circumstances of Cæsar's triumph. Casca, the "blunt fellow," will at first give only short prose answers to the verse questions, but eventually consents to elaborate his story:

> I can as well be hang'd as tell the manner of it. It was mere foolery; I did not mark it. I saw Mark Antony offer him a crown—yet 'twas not a crown neither, 'twas one of these coronets—and, as I told you, he put it by once; but for all that, to my thinking, he would fain have had it. Then he offered it to him again; then he put it by again; but to my thinking, he was very loath to lay his fingers off it. And then he offered it the third time. He put it the third time by; and still as he refus'd it, the rabblement hooted, and clapp'd their chopt hands, and threw up their sweaty nightcaps, and uttered such a deal of stinking breath because Cæsar refus'd the crown that it had, almost, chok'd Cæsar; for he swoonded and fell down at it. And for mine own part, I durst not laugh, for fear of opening my lips and receiving the bad air. (I, ii, 235–252)

The degradation of Cæsar's character proceeds systematically. Cassius tells of his weakness; Cæsar himself returns from the course and displays his arrogance; and finally

Casca comes to tell the comedy of the crown in such terms as move Brutus and persuade Cassius that a new conspirator has appeared. His words carry special weight because of their simplicity. He seems perfectly disinterested; he is not yet one of the conspirators. While Brutus and Cassius have been discussing the necessity for action in theoretical terms, Casca has seen the crown actually offered, and now comes to tell his friends that the time for action grows short. No formal oration in verse could achieve this end more effectively than Casca's rough prose. This speech, which so thoroughly reduces Cæsar's heroic dimensions, marks Shakespeare's first extended use of prose for satire and denigration. Such prose appears in *Troilus and Cressida*, and will presently be used by Hamlet in conversation with Rosencrantz and Guildenstern, and by Iago.

The play's great prose speech is Brutus' justification of the murder of Cæsar. The crowd demands an explanation and appears to be willing to listen to rational argument, as is indicated by the departure of some of the men with Cassius, to hear his reasons and to compare them with those of Brutus. It becomes evident that Cassius' rhetoric was, ultimately, no more persuasive than Brutus', although only the latter speaker is heard. Brutus opens, characteristically, with an injunction to the audience to hear him out:

Be patient till the last.

Romans, countrymen, and lovers, hear me for my cause, and be silent, that you may hear. Believe me for mine honour, and have respect to mine honour, that you may believe. Censure me in your wisdom, and awake your senses, that you may the better judge. If there be any in this assembly, any dear friend of Cæsar's, to him I say that Brutus' love to Cæsar was no less than his. If then that friend demand why Brutus rose against Cæsar, this is my answer: Not that I lov'd Cæsar less, but that I lov'd Rome more. Had you rather Cæsar were living, and die all slaves, than that Cæsar were dead, to live all freemen? As Cæsar lov'd me, I weep for him; as he was fortunate, I rejoice at it; as he was valiant, I honour him; but—as he was ambitious, I slew him. There is tears for his love; joy for his fortune; honour for his valour; and death for his ambition. Who is here so base that would be a bondman? If any, speak; for him have I offended. Who is here so rude that would not be a Roman? If any, speak; for him have I offended. Who is here so vile that will not love his country? If any, speak; for him have I offended. I pause for a reply.

. . . .

Then none have I offended. I have done no more to Cæsar than you shall do to Brutus. The question of his death is enroll'd in the Capitol; his glory not extenuated, wherein he was worthy; nor his offences enforc'd, for which he suffered death. . . . . Here comes his body, mourn'd by Mark Antony, who, though he had no hand in his death, shall receive the benefit of his dying, a place in the common-wealth, as which of you shall not? With this I depart, that, as I slew my best lover for the good of Rome, I have the same dagger for my-self when it shall please my country to need my death. (III, ii, 12–52)

Brutus deals with his audience as though explaining his action to another patrician in the Senate, first calling for belief in his honor, then protesting the disinterestedness of his part in the conspiracy, outlining Cæsar's merits and faults, and lastly promising Rome his own death when she may need it. Brutus' amazing insensitivity is better seen in this speech—in which he comes into closest touch with the Roman plebs—than anywhere else in the play. He is about to leave when he asks his audience to remain for Antony's speech. If he were to listen a little more closely to the plebeians, he might have certain qualms about the success of his explanation, for the Third Plebeian can yet say of him: "Let him be Cæsar." But Brutus is content that reason has triumphed.

If the speech of Brutus is quiet, reasonable, and logical Antony's speech is, of course, opposed to it in every possible way. Where Brutus is calm, Antony is impassioned; where Brutus pays honest tribute to Cæsar, Antony gives Brutus the lie with his cunningly repeated epithet, "honourable"; where Brutus appeals to reason, Antony befuddles his listeners with false logic. Antony begins artfully with a kind of parody of Brutus' style; but his calm hides rage, his praise is a mockery, and he speedily drops the disguise.

The clear-cut opposition of Brutus' prose and Antony's verse is one of Shakespeare's most cunningly contrived effects; nowhere does he contrast character more tellingly than in this scene. The mob is there—this time, be it noted, not speaking prose—to register promptly the changing shades of opinion. Prose and verse are, in this contest, made to show their most characteristic qualities, reason and emotion. Given the character of the mob as shown in the first scene of the play, its decision cannot come as a surprise.

This scene is followed at once by the sinister episode of Cinna the Poet (III, iii), who explains, in four lines of verse, that he has wandered strangely from his home, in the middle of the night and against his will, after dreaming of Cæsar. Set upon by the plebeians, he answers their questions jokingly, remaining unaware until the last moment that they are out for blood. The Second Plebeian's irritation with Cinna's supposed slight on marriage seems to warn the poet, who continues to reply in prose, but more directly. The plebeians are eager to murder Cinna as soon as they learn his name, although they admit knowing that he is not the conspirator. The stupid mob of the first scene becomes the furious mob which Antony can arouse to action, and now the murderous mob that kills Cinna for his name alone. The mob appears almost to have the personality of a single character, a personality which is not developed but revealed by successive events. It is no longer the clownish horde that followed Jack Cade, but a sinister and malign being.

Shakespeare's sparing use of prose in *Julius Cæsar* emphasizes the precision of the effects he achieves with it: the coolness of Brutus' unemotional self-justification, contrasted with Antony's brilliant and provocative harangue;

the fickleness, stupidity, and gross brutality of the mob; Casca's blunt contempt for Cæsar's histrionic heroics. The success of these effects is directly related to the economy with which they are devised.

6. *Hamlet*

Falstaff is Shakespeare's greatest creation in comic prose, Hamlet in tragic prose. Falstaff speaks prose because he must; verse is impossible for him. Hamlet, on the other hand, speaks some of the finest verse in all literature. His use of prose, then, springs from certain traits of his character and from the exigencies of his predicament. The interaction of these forces is responsible for both the quantity and quality of his prose. Hamlet, the brilliant young courtier, with rich intellectual endowments, is driven by the tragic fate of his father and the usurpation of his throne to put on the disguise of madness, the "antic disposition" in which he can safely give free rein to the melancholy and disillusion that have mastered him. Prose is for Shakespeare the language of melancholy, of cynical and caustic wit, and above all of madness. Hamlet shields himself with his prose; but it should not be supposed that the disguise alone explains the prose, or Edward Rowland Sill would be correct in assuming that Hamlet speaks prose when he is insincere and verse when he is sincere.[55] So oversimplified an analysis is meaningless; the very essence of Hamlet's camouflage lies in its ambiguity, its subtle confusion of truth and falsehood. Hamlet speaks both nonsense and cold fact in his apparent ravings. His disguise must obtain for him an immunity in which he can speak the truth by voicing his suspicions and grievances. The confusion which the "antic disposition" produces in its beholders is one of its most formidable weapons. Polonius finds in it the extreme of love-melancholy; the Queen, grief for the dead king and displeasure with her remarriage. Claudius is shrewder, but not yet resolved on a course of action. Hamlet has won time in these opening skirmishes by bewildering his opponents.

Hamlet's prose, however, does more than create confusion; it also contributes to the audience's understanding of his own confusion. His melancholy, for all that he uses it to throw his enemy off the track, is not therefore less genuine. His cynicism affords him a shield against Rosencrantz and Guildenstern. But he also uses prose with Horatio, from whom he has nothing to hide or fear. At the heart of his prose is an equivocation between appearance and reality, between the truth disguised from others and the truth that will make itself heard against its speaker's own will.

Prose makes its first important appearance in II, ii. Polonius sends the King and Queen away, remaining behind to question Hamlet, who mocks him quite openly, sprinkling his "mad" speeches with hints that support the love-madness theory. He makes so little effort to veil himself that Polonius twice comments in asides on the keenness of Hamlet's replies. Hamlet can permit himself such audacity in dealing with a man whom he despises and who has already convinced himself of the correctness of his theory.

The nature of Hamlet's conversation with Rosencrantz and Guildenstern is quite different. Polonius is a fool; the old friends from the university may not be very much more intelligent, but they are certainly more redoubtable foes. Hamlet therefore follows their lead in making satirical comments on the state of the world, but soon directs them back to Denmark and himself. He embarrasses them by exposing the motive of their visit, and proceeds to tell them why they have been sent for:

I will tell you why. So shall my anticipation prevent your discovery and your secrecy to the King and Queen moult no feather. I have of late, —but wherefore I know not—lost all my mirth, forgone all custom of exercises; and indeed, it goes so heavily with my disposition that this goodly frame, the earth, seems to me a sterile promontory; this most excellent canopy, the air, look you, this brave o'erhanging firmament, this majestical roof fretted with golden fire—why, it appeareth no other thing to me than a foul and pestilent congregation of vapours. What a piece of work is a man! how noble in reason! how infinite in faculties! in form and moving how express and admirable! in action how like an angel! in apprehension how like a god! the beauty of the world, the paragon of animals! And yet to me what is this quintessence of dust? Man delights not me—no, nor woman neither, though by your smiling you seem to say so. (II, ii, 304–323)

Nothing he says is false—except for five words, "but wherefore I know not," which reveal his ruse to us.

A new theme is introduced, that of the players, and Hamlet welcomes it gladly. Hamlet's melancholy, but a moment ago, soared to a lyric height; now he is delighted to immerse himself in theatrical gossip about the children's companies. For he is above all an actor, as Mark Van Doren has so well insisted,[56] and he will presently be capable of introducing an enchanting, somewhat irrelevant, and inexcusably extended disquisition on the art of acting—the dramatic point of which disappears when the speech which occasions it is not spoken. He is not really very much interested in pursuing the discussion with Rosencrantz and Guildenstern, and effectively silences them by speaking once more of Denmark and of his own situation. He will the more eagerly discuss plays and acting with the players themselves, after he has again played the madman at Polonius' reëntrance.

The encounter with the players brings into sharp relief the double contrast of prose and verse in this scene. Shakespeare not only opposes prose to verse, but also verse to verse. He has already used such a device in *A Midsummer Night's Dream*, contrasting the lovers' blank verse and the fairies' incantation-verse. But in *A Midsummer Night's Dream* the differences in verse-form as well as in the content of the speeches simplified the contrast; in *Hamlet*, both the players' lines and Hamlet's are in blank verse, both are passionate, highly emotional tirades. What, then, distinguishes the Pyrrhus-speech from "Oh, what a rogue and peasant slave am I!"? The most striking characteristics of the player's monologue, whether or not it be taken as a specific parody of the grand Marlovian style, are a deliberate stiffness, artificiality, and antiquatedness. It is dated verse, and Shakespeare expected his audience to find it dated, and to think Hamlet's reaction all the more startling. The Pyrrhus-speech, out of context, is heavy, old-fashioned, and even ludicrous. But it moves Hamlet to a passionate soul-searching in Shakespeare's most mature and colloquial blank verse. The Pyrrhus-speech is given a setting that is both prosaic and comic; nothing could be better calculated to bring out all that is lame, exaggerated, and unreal in the player's verse. If it were the only verse in the scene, one might perhaps consider it merely comic. But the dramatic point of the interpolation lies in the motive and cue which it gives Hamlet for his own great verse soliloquy; Hamlet rages because he cannot find in his own griefs the incentive to action, whereas the player can be utterly overwhelmed by a mere fiction.

The threefold division, whose boundaries are formally marked off in this scene by the use of prose and two kinds of verse, is the following: prose establishes the purely realistic and material frame of action, in the courtiers' light conversation; the player's verse brings an intrusion from the doubly unreal world of the theatre; and Hamlet's final soliloquy returns to the world in which the true spiritual action of the play takes place, the world of Hamlet's mind.

Following this complex arrangement of prose and verse comes the simple and powerful prose episode in III, i. The King and Polonius have hidden themselves, leaving Ophelia to draw out Hamlet. The latter enters and speaks the celebrated soliloquy in which, among other things, he gives abundant proof of his sanity. He then becomes aware of Ophelia's presence and plunges at once into a prose which counterfeits madness. He probably suspects that he is being overheard; in any case, he will not take Ophelia into his confidence.

The coarseness and fury of Hamlet's speeches in this scene may proceed from his disgust at seeing Ophelia made her father's tool, or from his fear that his feigned insanity is no longer believed. Both elements are surely present; but, dominating them, is the spirit of cynicism, reduction, denigration, which appeared first in the scene with Rosencrantz and Guildenstern. The world is a sterile promontory, says Hamlet; retire permanently from it. Hamlet expresses himself too clearly, for the King can say

> Love? his affections do not that way tend;
> Nor what he spake, though it lack'd form a little,
> Was not like madness. (III, i, 170–172)

The dramatic extraneousness of the speech to the Players (III, ii) is, of course, patent. Be it noted, however, how well the speech contributes to the picture of Hamlet as actor: it is brilliantly contrived, giving him the opportunity to illustrate the faults against which he warns. It moves easily from the longer and more general injunctions—"Speak the speech, I pray you, as I pronounced it to you, trippingly on the tongue" (how far the Euphuistic rhetoric has come since Lyly!)—to the short, pungent ejaculation of disgust—"It out-Herods Herod." It is magnificent prose, and certainly not altogether without dramatic point, for Hamlet is about to expound the message of his play. And one need not be surprised to find mingled with the passion of the revenger the professional pride of the stage-manager.

Between these last words to the actors and the performance of *The Murder of Gonzago* comes a short interlude in verse. Hamlet can address Horatio in verse, the language of his soul, because he knows himself to be in the presence of the one man from whom he needs to hide nothing, the man "that is not passion's slave." This trust is the burden of his speech, in which he shows himself, for a fleeting instant, the courteous gentleman which the action of his tragedy will not allow him to be. He is vouchsafed for a moment the privilege of appearing in his essential self; but, again, "I must be idle," he says, and plays the madman once more for his uncle.

The play of Gonzago is in a rhymed verse which is yet more stilted than the earlier interpolated verse. This increased artificiality effectively sets off Hamlet's prose comments. Hamlet gaily interprets and discusses the stiff, archaic tragedy for the one man who needs no gloss at all to help him understand.

From this point on, Hamlet becomes increasingly careless of his disguise; indeed, he appears to retain it, after its usefulness is at an end, solely for the pleasure it affords him. He makes insane quibbles with Rosencrantz und Guildenstern, when they come to summon him to his mother, but does so for his own amusement. The parable of the recorders is not too difficult for them to comprehend, nor is it meant to be. The twitting of Polonius, immediately afterwards, is mere extravagance. Hamlet has at last arrived at a pitch of ecstasy in which he feels himself capable of anything, and, in a concluding verse speech, proclaims his intention to act.

In his exchanges with Rosencrantz and Guildenstern (IV, ii) and with the King (IV, iii), Hamlet still plays the madman, but contemptuously, scarcely troubling to veil his sarcasm in wild words. He is aware that the voyage to England is one from which he is not intended to return; the comedy is all but ended. His former friends do not understand his jesting. The King does, but pretends ignorance in order to force Hamlet into the protective custody of the trip to England. The King is a clever and dangerous opponent, as Hamlet well knows, and this final conversation before Hamlet's departure is a measuring of swords.

After so much feigned madness, the genuine distraction of Ophelia is particularly shocking. The snatches of song and the pathetic prose fragment produce an effect beside which Hamlet's fiction of insanity at once appears the calculated work of a skilled actor. Hamlet is always regarded by the King and the rest with fear, suspicion, and bewilderment; they make some attempt to humor him and to maintain the semblance of a serious conversation. No such treatment is accorded Ophelia, beyond the King's heavy and abortive efforts to speak to her as to a child. At her first exit, the King promptly analyzes the causes of her distraction in concise and pertinent language which is at the opposite pole from the madness of Ophelia. At her reëntrance, Laertes apostrophizes her in extravagant terms, but only once addresses her directly. A double contrast is established by her calm demeanor and his fury, by her gentle prose and his ranting verse. Mad prose or not, Ophelia's speech seems at least as sane as her brother's raving.

Two letters from Hamlet are read aloud in the last two scenes of Act IV. The first letter, to Horatio, is prefaced by the Sailor's few lines of prose; it is short and to the point, informative and friendly. The second, to the King, announces Hamlet's return and his desire to see the King; but its two sentences recreate suddenly the contemptuous and deliberately mystifying manner of Hamlet in the presence of his enemies. This gage thrown to the King illustrates admirably how the prose letter can be made to intrude into a scene. The King and Laertes, now friends, find their content at Hamlet's supposed death rudely shattered by the very fact of the letter's arrival. The text of the letter gives them whatever additional incentive they need to plot the manner of his death.

The prose of the gravediggers' scene accomplishes several functions at almost the same time. The clown's callous joking reveals that they are preparing a suicide's grave; since the news of Ophelia's death has come at the close of the preceding scene, the connection is not difficult to make. Thus a powerful ironic point is given to Hamlet's variations on the *ubi sunt* theme; his sudden recognition of the fact that he is an involuntary mourner at Ophelia's grave at once transforms the entire mood and direction of the scene.

The prose section of the graveyard scene follows a definite scheme: the clowns supply the information which will explain the later action; the clown's song and work inspire first Hamlet's ironic fantasies on the skulls, and the subsequent dialogue gives him information about the corpse for whom the grave is intended. Hamlet is led by his meditation on Yorick and Alexander to conclude his prose speech with a quatrain:

> Imperious Cæsar, dead and turn'd to clay
> Might stop a hole to keep the wind away.
> O, that that earth which kept the world in awe
> Should patch a wall t' expel the winter's flaw! (V, i, 236–239)

as he did earlier, after the brusque termination of *The Murder of Gonzago* (III, ii). The sudden impulse to rhyme reveals Hamlet in a queerly excited and humorous mood, induced by his speculations on death and by the identification of the chapfallen skull as that of his childhood friend. It is at this moment that the funeral procession arrives. In the ensuing action, Hamlet speaks only verse. And now, ironically, although Hamlet takes no pains to disguise himself, both his entirely true statements and his burlesque rant are taken as evidence of his madness. When he realizes how little chance he has of making himself understood, he reverts for two lines to his mock-lunatic vein and leaves.

Osric's entrance in the final scene is the cue for the last prose in the play. Here is a burlesque of the affected courtier, who couches the simplest ideas in the most absurd and extravagant jargon, yet who cannot even understand this jargon when he hears it from another. In such elaborate style are the arrangements for the fencing bout concluded; and the effect of this interlude is to present these facts without calling undue attention to them. Hamlet's amused and contemptuous treatment of the waterfly helps to divert Hamlet's own suspicion.

The transition from this dialogue to the bout itself is effected in two short passages of prose: the conversation with the lord who is sent ahead to confirm the arrangements which Osric has broached, and the last speeches between Hamlet and Horatio. Hamlet's lines in private with his friend are the noble statement of his resignation to a known and yet uncertain fate:

> If it be now, 'tis not to come; if it be not to come, it will be now; if it be not now, yet it will come: the readiness is all. Since no man knows aught of what he leaves, what is't to leave betimes? Let be. (V, ii, 231–235)

It is appropriate that this fatalism, the ultimate distillation of so much hesitation and thinking, should be in prose; its expression in the graveyard-scene links these two last prose-scenes. From this time until his death, Hamlet will appear completely himself at last, as capable in action as he has been incapable in the contemplation of action. The time for thinking is past, but this idea too must be expressed in the language of thought.

The prose of *Hamlet* is intimately associated with the whole theme of madness in the play. Prose is at once Hamlet's protective disguise and his medium of communication with a suspect world. But it is also, by extension, the language of that world in its relation to him. "The time is out of joint," and therefore verse, the rightful language of Hamlet in normal relation to his world, becomes impossible both for him and for that dreadfully transformed world. Hamlet speaks verse to the court *before* he puts on the antic disposition and *after* he has at last decided to act. In the interim, he can speak verse only to himself or to his trusted friend.

The interplay of prose and verse in *Hamlet* of necessity depends on the use made of prose. For all the prose in the play is spoken or inspired by Hamlet. Hence the primary determinant of the greatest part of the prose is Hamlet himself; the deliberate introduction of prose from without for the purpose of heightening a specific dramatic situation hardly occurs at all in this play. Contrasts within a scene exist, to be sure, but they exist because of the opposition between Hamlet and some other character or characters. The use of prose for dramatic contrast thus grows out of the use of prose for delineation of character.

But what fundamentally underlies the prose of Hamlet himself? It is a bitter, disillusioned view of the world. Hamlet explicitly states that the earth has become for him a "sterile promontory," the very air "a foul and pestilent congregation of vapours." Through Hamlet's eyes we see the world thus reduced; and the prose in which he reduces it is trenchant and corrosive. It has already appeared as the prose of denigration in Casca's speech on Cæsar; it is the language in which Thersites and Apemantus rant. Verse enlarges the world by generalizing and universalizing particular instances; prose contracts the world by showing the baseness of the apparently great and noble.

In composing *Hamlet*, Shakespeare may well have had before him the example of the additions to *The Spanish Tragedie* when he gave Hamlet satirical tirades in prose. There can be little question but that John Marston, in his turn, had *Hamlet* in mind when he used the prose of satire and denigration as part of the disguise for his Malevole, the hero of *The Malcontent* (1604). At one point in the opening scene of the play, Malevole, left alone with a trusted friend, drops his disguise and speaks verse in his own character of Altofronto; when a third person enters, he returns to prose. The change is strikingly emphasized by the stage direction: "Malevole shifteth his speech."[57] At the end of the play, when Malevole stands revealed before all the characters as Altofronto, he speaks only verse.

In the prose of reduction and denigration, which has its finest and fullest expression in *Hamlet*, lies Shakespeare's major development of the prose convention. Webster, Tourneur, and Ford followed Shakespeare's lead, and the success of Webster's characterization of Flamineo is a measure of the profundity of Shakespeare's influence.

7. *Othello*

Iago dominates most of the prose in *Othello* (1604), either speaking it himself or causing others to speak it. It is one manifestation—and a very important one—of the character Iago has created as a disguise for himself: "honest Iago," the blunt soldier who speaks truth without counting the cost and who cannot prevail on his conscience to let him remain silent. The cynical realism of prose lends its weight to this disguise. But prose is not Iago's true language; whenever he is alone, he drops into the verse of the Machiavellian villain, the verse of Richard III or of Edmund. Iago's bluntness is the deceiving candor Cornwall pretends to find in Kent.

Iago's prose, at its first appearance, is characteristically scurrilous. He and Roderigo stand in the street below Brabantio's house (I,i) and give the alarm. Iago presses Roderigo on to shout, but promptly outshouts him, bewildering and infuriating Brabantio with his obscenities. Roderigo reveals himself and tries to speak courteously to the old man, but Iago breaks in rudely in prose:

> Zounds, sir, you are one of those that will not serve God if the devil bid you. Because we come to do you service, and you think we are ruffians, you'll have your daughter cover'd with a Barbary horse; you'll have your nephews neigh to you; you'll have coursers for cousins, and gennets for germans...
>
> I am one, sir, that come to tell you your daughter and the Moor are now making the beast with two backs. (I, i, 108–114, 116–118)

and flees before his identity can be discovered.

Othello is an enclosed play; most of its action takes place in a series of interiors whose atmosphere is heavy and charged. To this effect the verse contributes in great measure; but prose reminds participants and spectators that there is another world without. In I, iii, Othello's successful plea has been heard, and the Duke attempts to comfort Brabantio with moralizing couplets on the value of patience; the old man's retort, likewise in couplets, sarcastically questions the value of such sentences. He ends with a single unrhymed line: "Beseech you, now to the affairs of state" (220), and the Duke, in prose, gives Othello his orders for the defense of Cyprus, the hard and businesslike tone of the prose recalling the danger to the State. Othello's request brings back verse for the discussion of his personal problem, and no more prose is heard until the company leaves, and Iago and Roderigo speak privately. Iago, in his most cynical vein, teases and insults the gallant out of his suicidal humour. The extent of his persuasiveness and of Roderigo's gullibility can be seen in Roderigo's ready acceptance of his arguments, immediately after having seen Othello and Desdemona together. Off goes Roderigo to collect his money, leaving Iago to formulate his plan of action in verse. Iago, by thus inheriting the scene, commands it; the same is true of the first and third scenes of the second act and of III, iii, all of which contribute to the impression that Iago is in complete possession of the action, and divert attention from the flimsiness of his plan.

While waiting for Othello's arrival (II, i), Desdemona, announcing her intention to beguile "the thing I am by seeming otherwise," drops into prose banter with Iago, who recites impromptu epigrams in doggerel. Othello restores verse, but Iago has already spoken a prose aside on Desdemona and Cassio; again the company departs, except for Iago and Roderigo, and the pattern of I, iii is duplicated: Iago pursues his sinister scheme in prose with his dupe, and presently indicates in a verse soliloquy the direction of his machinations. Prose is firmly established as the language of intrigue and degradation, masquerading as cynical and soldier-like frankness.

The Herald's prose proclamation (II, ii) shows the normal convention in operation. Scene iii opens with the exit of Othello and Desdemona. Iago's entrance brings prose; he baits Cassio with rough allusions to Desdemona's beauty, and Cassio, unwilling to seem a prig, makes cautious replies. Iago fills in the implausibly short space of Cassio's absence with a verse speech. The drinking-scene, again, is in prose; as soon as Cassio is gone, however, Iago seizes the opportunity to moralize in verse on Cassio's alleged failing. The fight and Cassio's banishment are naturally in verse, and again Iago and a dupe—this time Cassio—are left alone. Cassio's prose grows out of his distress and confusion; Iago, as before, is the cynical, friendly counsellor, persuading his gull that reputation is of no more account than virtue, that Othello's reproof is a "punishment more in policy than in malice," and that Desdemona's voice will procure Cassio his reinstatement. Iago soliloquizes in verse until Roderigo comes. Iago has no time to answer his importunate fool in prose, but sends him packing with a few lines of verse, anxious to get on with his intrigue.

The Clown's interlude with the musicians (III, i) relaxes the tension momentarily, before the violence to come. His next appearance (III, iv) finds the tragic action well advanced.

Othello's mad prose and trance are the symbolic and literal manifestations of his breakdown. He is completely beside himself. When he recovers, he is made to watch (but not to hear) Iago's conversations with Cassio and with Bianca. All Othello's interjections are in prose; and one must consider the effect of hearing such prose from a man who until now has spoken only verse of a remarkable brilliance and splendor. He has literally become a raging animal. Othello is made to undergo mental and physical disintegration simultaneously; when he recovers his senses, he, the noble lord, must become an eavesdropper. And the dialogue with Iago sees Othello ranging from brute savagery ("I will chop her into messes!") to something little short of grotesque comedy. Against this dreadful background is played out the parody of an official welcome to Lodovico.

Desdemona, thunderstruck and "half asleep" after her interview with Othello (IV, ii), seeks advice of Emilia and Iago, ultimately begging Iago to intercede for her with Othello. At this moment the half-forgotten Roderigo returns to complain in prose of Iago's neglect. Iago replies in short sentences, recognizing that Roderigo is no longer a treasury, but a potential source of great mischief. He fobs him off with hastily invented pretexts, busily improvising a scheme to dispose of him permanently. Iago does not, as is his custom, conclude with a soliloquy; he will recite it, instead, during the scene of Roderigo's murder.

The last scene of the act does not advance the action, and

it is also the last scene in the mixed form. The exchange of courtesies at the beginning is cut short by Othello's peremptory prose command:

> Get you to bed on th' instant. I will be return'd forthwith. Dispatch your attendant there. Look't be done. (IV, iii, 7–9)

The scene now moves slowly to its full close. Desdemona is resigned; she sings her song, and yet she must ask Emilia whether women exist who could deceive their husbands. Emilia jokes with her in prose, Desdemona returning grave verse answers. In the middle of her last cynical statement, Emilia shifts to verse to inveigh against husbands who force their wives to adultery. Desdemona cannot argue, but only pray. Emilia's prose mocks the whole tragic motive of the play immediately before the catastrophe.

The sinister voice of Iago, the *faux bonhomme*, mocking, persuasive, appealing to realism and preaching cynicism, systematically blackening and reducing the beautiful and virtuous characters, speaks the greater part of the play's prose. The other familiar manifestations of the convention appear, but fade in importance before the technique of reduction and denigration. Indeed, *Othello* is the perfect example of this use of the convention; for, by reducing Othello's world to a sterile promontory, Iago finally demolishes it altogether. The convention is a symbol and microcosm of the entire play.

8. *King Lear*

The prose of *King Lear* (1605–6) performs many and varied functions: it establishes a tone of cynical realism in the dialogue of Goneril and Regan; a tone of bluff frankness in the prose disguise of Kent; the Machiavellianism of Edmund; the madness of Lear and the pretended madness of Edgar; and it ultimately combines with verse to produce, in the extraordinary harmonies of the trial scene, a blending of forms that is unique in Shakespeare.

The opening passage of the play's first scene is in prose and seems, at first, to be outright exposition, for Gloucester's and Kent's speeches look forward to Lear's division of the kingdom; but Kent's question about Edmund spurs Gloucester on to an unnecessarily precise explanation of his son's illegitimacy. The entrance of Lear and the court cuts short the conversation. The body of the scene is in verse, as befits its serious matter; but the short prose epilogue moves from the serious to the sinister. Goneril and Regan remain behind to discuss, in the most practical and realistic of terms, the meaning and implications of Lear's actions. The abrupt change from verse to prose intensifies the cold calculation of their remarks; the accuracy of their analysis and their perfect understanding of their father's hasty anger reveal in a short passage the darkness of their characters and intentions.

The next scene begins with Edmund's verse eulogy of illegitimacy. He adroitly calls his father's attention to the forged letter by his clumsiness in hiding it. The ensuing dialogue, in which Edgar is betrayed, is in prose; Edmund feigns, in turn, politeness, innocence, and a soothing reasonableness. He goads Gloucester as far as he dares with his own pretended proofs and then offers to engage Edgar in such conversation as will confirm his guilt to an eavesdropper. Gloucester will not have this: "He cannot be such a monster," and Edmund, following the wind, quickly agrees: "Nor is not, sure." Edmund watches his father leave, and soliloquizes drily in prose on the latter's astrological interpretation of his son's supposed villainy, cynically offering himself as an example in contradiction. Edgar's entrance cuts across this prose monologue, and the legitimate son is now hoodwinked like the father. Edmund is left alone on the stage at the end to summarize his policy in verse, rounding out the symmetry of the scene. The Machiavellian plan is first stated in verse; then prose is called in for the accomplishment of the two deceptions, and the contriver compliments himself in verse on his success.

Kent enters (I, iv) in a disguise the purpose of which he explains briefly in verse. He speaks prose in conversation with Lear as part of that disguise; prose lends a certain common quality to his native bluntness and thus contributes to the preservation of his incognito. The scene moves forward unhurriedly, although its direction soon becomes unmistakable. Oswald is rude; the Knight makes Lear realize that Goneril and her servants have shown a marked lack of courtesy; Oswald returns and is chastised; and the Fool rings a dozen changes in prose and song on his master's ill-advised abdication. Thus, by a series of short prose episodes, the action is advanced to the point where Goneril's entrance brings verse and a naked opposition of wills. The all-licens'd Fool links the two parts of the scene with his mocking interjections and warns Lear (I, v) that he may expect nothing better at Regan's hands. Lear joins the Fool in prose, trying to calm himself, but twice breaks out again in verse:

> To take't again perforce! Monster ingratitude!...
> O, let me not be mad, not mad, sweet heaven!
> Keep me in temper; I would not be mad! (I, v, 43, 49–50)

Kent and Oswald meet at Gloucester's castle (II, ii), where Kent at once provokes a fight. Edmund parts them, and Cornwall restores order with verse. Kent cuts across Oswald's verse explanation with a prose tirade, after which he himself justifies his attack in verse. Angered by Cornwall's aspersions on the sincerity of his bluntness, he begins an overelaborate parody of courtly verse style. He answers Cornwall's puzzled "What mean'st thou by this?" with

To go out of my dialect, which you discommend so much. I know, sir, I am no flatterer. He that beguil'd you in a plain accent was a plain knave, which, for my part, I will not be, though I should win your displeasure to entreat me to't. (II, ii, 115–120)

Kent's prose makes his bluntness appear the more credible by contrast with his own mock-hypocritical verse. But Oswald's own version of that verse carries the day.

In Lear's encounter with Regan (II, iv) and in his first scene on the heath (III, ii) only the Fool speaks prose, removing himself from direct participation in the events he witnesses. His comments retain their ironic appositeness, but they are uttered as by a creature apart, barely heard and not at all heeded. In the moment of Lear's submission, however, the King's thoughts turn again to the Fool.

Gloucester is once more betrayed by Edmund in III, iii, the pattern following that of their earlier scenes. Gloucester confides, in prose, his plan to aid Lear, and tells the news of the invasion. Edmund, left alone, summarizes in verse the progress of his fortunes.

The prose of madness enters the play in the following scene with the disguised Edgar's first wild words, which drive the Fool from the hovel. Edgar's appearance first excites Lear's sympathy because the old King fancies he may find a fellow-sufferer in the madman, and he questions him in verse:

> What, have his daughters brought him to this pass?
> Couldst thou save nothing? Didst thou give them all?
> (III, iv, 65–66)

and calls down plagues on those daughters. Edgar's long speech seems to turn Lear's mind from this fancy, for now he sees in the poor madman not one whose daughters have brought him to this pass, but nothing less than his own image:

Why, thou wert better in thy grave than to answer with thy uncover'd body this extremity of the skies. Is man no more than this? Consider him well. Thou ow'st the worm no silk, the beast no hide, the sheep no wool, the cat no perfume. Ha! Here's three on's are sophisticated! Thou art the thing itself; unaccommodated man is no more but such a poor, bare, forked animal as thou art. Off, off, you lendings! Come, unbutton here. (III, iv, 105–114)

Gloucester comes to lead them all to his farmhouse; he revives the theme of ingratitude when Lear has at last momentarily forgotten it. The latter part of this scene, like the greater part of scene vi, dissolves into a strange mixture of verse, prose, and song. This mixture is all that makes the strength of these scenes and keeps them dramatically possible, as Harley Granville-Barker has said:

> The dramatic vitality of these scenes lies largely in this variety and balance of orchestration; their emotional strain might be intolerable without it.[58]

The dialogue of the "trial-scene" (IV, vi) passes almost beyond sense altogether:

> The sound of the dialogue matters almost more than its meaning. Poor Tom and the Fool chant antiphonally; Kent's deep and kindly tones tell against the higher, agonized, weakening voice of Lear. But the chief significance is in the show. Where Lear, such a short while since, sat in his majesty, there sit the Fool and the outcast, with Kent whom he banished beside them; and he, witless, musters his failing strength to beg justice upon a joint-stool. Was better justice done, the picture ironically asks, when he presided in majesty and sanity and power?[59]

The Fool, at the beginning of this, his last scene, recovers himself somewhat and jokes in his traditional style. The first effect is one of relief, now that the fools and madmen are sheltered at last; but the Fool's question is given a dreadful turn by Lear, and the comedy is bound still more strongly to the tragic whole.

The departure of the group for Dover, on Gloucester's order, leaves Edgar behind to say the last word on the terrible scene just past. There is great dramatic art in this conclusion, which brings forward the half-naked wretch to speak in sententious couplets whose orderly precision is at the farthest remove from his appearance and from his mad gabbling during the scene just past.

The short prose scene between Cornwall and Edmund (III, v), which separates the two mad scenes, looks forward, in its combination of treachery and cold fury, to the horrors of Gloucester's blinding. The first dozen lines of the latter scene (III, vii) are likewise in prose: Cornwall's commands, Goneril and Regan's bloody suggestions, and Cornwall's ironically solicitous farewell to Goneril and Edmund ("The revenges we are bound to take upon your traitorous father are not fit for your beholding"). The dreadful business is quickly and efficiently consummated in verse.

Edgar's leading of his blind father begins in IV, i. It has been suggested that his insane outburst (lines 56-64) is spurious, and it may well be. He has already told us in an aside, "I cannot daub it further." He has no need to convince Gloucester of his madness, and the speech itself is uninspired embroidery of his superb raving in the hovel. A further indication that the disguise is in process of transformation is the fact that Edgar speaks only verse when he pretends to lead Gloucester to the cliff (IV, vi), a fact which arouses the old man's suspicions.

To Edgar and his father now comes the mad Lear, his speech wavering between verse and prose. These last outbursts of Lear in his mad state are the most violent; for his most shocking effects, Shakespeare draws on sexual themes, and makes the King grow almost inarticulate with disgust:

> Down from the waist they are Centaurs,
> Though women all above.
> But to the girdle do the gods inherit,
> Beneath is all the fiend's.

There's hell, there's darkness, there's the sulphurous pit; burning, scalding, stench, consumption. Fie, fie, fie! pah, pah! Give me an ounce of civet, good apothecary, to sweeten my imagination. There's money for thee. (IV, vi, 126–134)

This speech may serve as a symbolic representation of Lear's breakdown, the verse becoming increasingly irregular and finally turning into prose; a listing of words and mere ejaculations of revulsion; lastly, an attempt to recover. Again, he returns from prose to verse. He trembles between madness and sanity; Edgar can say of him

> O, matter and impertinency mix'd!
> Reason in madness! (IV, vi, 178–179)

Lear summons up dignity and verse to remind Cordelia's man that he is a king; then shouts two lines of prose and runs out.

Oswald comes upon Gloucester and Edgar, who assumes a countryman's dialect. Oswald challenges father and son, speaking the verse which denotes his pride in his station. Edgar takes his cue from Oswald's contemptuous "bold peasant." There is an interval of calm after the steward's death, while Edgar searches his pockets; but it is broken by the reading of the prose letter, which shows Edgar his course.

The last significant prose in the play consists of a few lines, epilogue to the scene of Lear's awakening (IV, vii). Kent and an anonymous gentleman are left on the stage after Lear and Cordelia have departed. Kent confirms the death of Cornwall and his replacement by Edmund; but to the rumor that he himself is with Edgar in Germany, he replies drily, "Report is changeable. 'Tis time to look about; the powers of the kingdom approach apace." (IV, vii, 92–94). From this point on, the play, except for the proclamation before the duel of Edmund and Edgar, resolves itself in verse.

The play's prose is associated with certain characters, but in every instance the dramatic situations in which those characters are involved give the key to their use of prose. And beyond them are the characters such as Edgar or Lear, to whom prose is not native, and who, under the force of circumstances, come to speak prose. The variety of the "orchestration," to borrow Granville-Barker's term, is infinite.

The apparent breakdown of the distinction between prose and verse, as in the scene of the mock trial, actually points not to a violation, but to a transcendence of the prose convention. Prose and verse are normally contrasted in Shakespeare's plays. But *King Lear*, while keeping the element of contrast (the Edmund-scenes against the Lear-scenes), introduces a new synthesis of forms, such as would have been impossible in the earlier plays, in which the distinction between forms is strongly marked; this synthesis in *King Lear* bears further witness to the breakdown of the distinction. Some of the play's blank verse is strikingly irregular, even without an admixture of prose. For another example of such a synthesis, one must look to Flamineo's death-speech in *The White Devil*. But Flamineo must make his own synthesis, whereas Shakespeare produces harmony by orchestrating his scene for several voices.

9. *Timon of Athens*

The use of prose in *Timon of Athens* poses some very curious problems. On the surface, the main lines are clear enough: *Timon of Athens* is a satirical play, whose prose is closely associated with its satire. The scoffer Apemantus speaks prose, as do the objects of his mockery when they speak with him. Timon, after his conversion, rails in prose in his turn against the false misanthrope. The short scenes in which Timon's servants vainly try to borrow money for their master employ prose in various ways.

So considered, the play is in no way extraordinary. Its prose is often very good, but as often flat and colorless, especially in such scenes as the last of I, i, where Apemantus is made to engage in a series of short, scathing little dialogues with Timon and divers flatterers. There is little imagination in the contriving of this scene, and no distinction in the writing. On the other hand, the play poses serious textual problems.

Timon of Athens mixes verse and prose with a carelessness that is entirely uncharacteristic of Shakespeare. It has seemed appropriate to insist on the deliberateness and careful planning which Shakespeare put into his use of prose and verse, and it is at least startling to find him mingling the forms in so cavalier a fashion. One cannot even guess at what he intended by it: it is even quite possible that he intended nothing at all, and that the text of *Timon of Athens* may not be susceptible of the same kind of criticism that one feels free to apply in the case of other plays.

Consider the following passage:

> *Timon.* O, Apemantus, you are welcome.
> *Apem.*   No,
>   You shall not make me welcome.
>   I come to have thee thrust me out of doors.
> *Timon.* Fie, th'art a churl; y'have got a humour there
>   Does not become a man; 'tis much to blame,
>   They say, my lords, *Ira furor brevis est*;

but yond man is ever angry. Go, let him have a table by himself; for he does neither affect company nor is he fit for't indeed.

> *Apem.* Let me stay at thine apperil, Timon. I come to observe; I give thee warning on't.

> *Timon.* I take no heed of thee. Th'art an Athenian, therefore welcome. I myself would have no power; prithee let my meat make thee silent.

> *Apem.* I scorn thy meat. 'Twould choke me, for I should ne'er flatter thee. O you gods, what a number of men eats Timon, and he sees them not! It grieves me to see so many dip their meat in one man's blood; and all the madness is, he cheers them up too.
>   I wonder men dare trust themselves with men,
>   Methinks they should invite them without knives:
>   Good for their meat, and safer for their lives.

There's much example for't. The fellow that sits next him now, parts bread with him, pledges the breath of him in a divided draught, is the readiest man to kill him. 'T has been proved. If I were a huge man, I should fear to drink at meals,

> Lest they should spy my windpipe's dangerous notes.
> Great men should drink with harness on their throats.

Timon. (*to a Lord who drinks to him*) My lord, in heart! and let the health go round.

2. Lord. Let it flow this way, my good lord.

Apem. Flow this way? A brave fellow! He keeps his tides well. Those healths will make thee and thy state look ill, Timon. Here's that which is too weak to be a sinner, honest water, which ne'er left man in the mire.

> This and my food are equals; there's no odds,
> Feasts are too proud to give thanks to the gods.

Apemantus' Grace

> Immortal gods, I crave no pelf,
> I pray for no man but myself.
> Grant I may never prove so fond
> To trust man on his oath or bond,
> Or a harlot for her weeping,
> Or a dog that seems a-sleeping,
> Or a keeper with my freedom,
> Or my friends, if I should need 'em.
> Amen. So fall to't.
> Rich men sin, and I eat root.
> > (*Eats and drinks.*)

Much good dich thy good heart, Apemantus! (I, ii, 23–74)

The first noteworthy point is Timon's passing from verse to prose within a single short speech. It may be argued that he is turning his attention from Apemantus to his other guests, but the shift is too violent to be explained away so easily. In any case, this explanation cannot serve for the next change, for Apemantus addresses first Timon and then the gods in prose. He now speaks three lines of verse, the second and third of which form a couplet. Five lines of prose follow, and the speech ends with another. After a brief interruption, Apemantus again speaks prose, a couplet, says his grace, and ends with a prose line.

The confusion of prose and verse may indicate that this is an unfinished or unrevised version of Apemantus' and Timon's speeches. A final version might have been entirely in verse. This suggestion cannot be offered too tentatively. Apemantus, like Thersites, is a prose speaker because he is a satirical commentator. His prose, like Thersites', is one of denigration and reduction; long verse speeches—soliloquies excepted—would be at odd variance with his character. Yet why does Apemantus speak verse at all? His verse lines are more moralizing in tone than even the prose with which they are interwoven. If he speaks any verse under circumstances which seem to require prose, he might speak more verse; he in fact does so, at the end of the scene:

> What a coil's here!
> Serving of becks and jutting-out of bums!
> I doubt whether their legs be worth the sums
> That are given for 'em. Friendship's full of dregs,
> Methinks false hearts should never have sound legs.
> Thus honest fools lay out their wealth on curtsies. (I, ii, 236–241)

(One wonders why the two couplets are followed by a single unrhymed line.) And Timon's reply causes Apemantus to speak not more verse, but prose.

It is possible, of course, that the passages quoted merely testify to the breakdown of distinctions between prose and verse that came with the Jacobean drama. The passage just quoted may be compared with Flamineo's dying speech in *The White Devil*, in which prose, rhymed verse, and blank verse are all used together. Although Webster himself differentiated the forms clearly, the fact that he could thus bring them all into one speech indicates that the formal distinctions —with their dramatic overtones—had become relatively weak. Shakespeare's confusion of forms may here produce a similar effect, but in his usual practice he distinguishes the forms with precision.

The danger of overlong speculation on *Timon of Athens* as a working manuscript is obvious. Parts of the play may have been sketched out in prose, to be turned into verse at some later date; it seems a plausible method of composition. One hardly dares apply any tentative conclusions from this evidence to Shakespeare's other plays. The chief argument against such procedure is the seeming state of completion of the plays. Until manuscripts of Shakespeare's plays in various stages of completion are found, his method must remain unknown. And a play as it appears in the First Folio is not the best evidence for the reconstruction of that method. It is nevertheless tempting to think that *Timon of Athens* may offer the unique glimpse of a Shakespearean play in the work-in-progress state. That the play is unfinished can scarcely be doubted. Professor Kittredge speaks for many scholars when he says that the play's "flaws and irregularities . . . are adequately explained by the obvious fact that Shakespeare never really finished the play."[60]

However jumbled an appearance the text as a whole presents, the arrangement of prose and verse in several scenes bears witness that the play is the product of Shakespeare's maturest period. Flaminius' interview with Lucullus (III, i) has a shift from prose to verse to mark Flaminius' sudden anger with the man who tries to bribe him to silence. The next scene is built on a similar pattern, with the First Stranger (who observes the action but does not participate in it) speaking the moralizing verse conclusion. Lucius speaks with Servilius and the strangers in prose, but indicates his surprise at the servant's request in two lines of verse.

The most fully developed scene involving an opposition of prose and verse is that of Timon's final banquet (III, vi). The prose dialogue of the two unidentified friends of Timon, by once more exposing their cupidity and ingratitude, looks forward to the dénouement; Timon enters and converses civilly with them, bids all the guests to their places, and speaks a grace in prose. Its dignity makes its profound misanthropy the more impressive. Beside it, the cynical jingle of Apemantus' grace is merely trivial. The uncovering of the dishes is Timon's cue for a long, fierce attack in verse, his last farewell to his flatterers. The language of the prose prayer is obscure to the guests; its insults are too generalized. No such criticism can be made of the verse speech, which reaches its mark with the unmistakable directness of the warm water. The confused prose of the departing guests mirrors their stupidity and venality. The vivid opposition of the parts of the scene to each other is intensified by the contrast of conversational prose to the set speech in prose, and of the latter to the violent verse.

The satirical character of *Timon of Athens* is the most important element influencing the use of prose. Some of the play's variations from the norm, in this respect, are to be understood as developments and elaborations by Shakespeare; others can probably be attributed to the fact that our text of the play is incomplete and unrevised.

10. *Macbeth*

The prose of *Macbeth* (1606), unlike that of *Hamlet*, depends upon no one character for its meaning and direction. It is, like every other element in this barest and starkest of Shakespeare's tragedies, employed primarily for dramatic purposes. The unrelieved economy of the play may, to be sure, be explained by hypotheses about the text, but no such discussion will be undertaken here; it must remain immaterial whether the text of the play is an acting version or identical with Shakespeare's manuscript. The fact that the play has been pruned of all superfluous material is of greater importance than the problem of assigning the editorial credit to the artistic imagination of the playwright or to the director's time schedule.

One consequence of this brevity and compression is an extremely sparing but effective use of prose. Four scenes in *Macbeth* contain prose; none of the four is entirely in prose, and the longest single passage does not exceed forty-five lines. Yet the deletion of these passages would be unthinkable. Three of the four are governed directly by the oldest prose conventions of the Elizabethan drama: a letter, a clown-scene, and a mad scene. They can be taken, moreover, as almost ideal illustrations of these conventional usages; and their use in *Macbeth* could not be more sophisticated or more pertinent dramatically.

Macbeth's letter has a double dramatic force: it recounts, briefly and vividly, events which the audience has already witnessed, and it provokes, with sinister speed, Lady Macbeth's resolute decision. Macbeth himself could not state the facts more powerfully than does his letter, as read aloud by his wife. He himself is rarely so articulate; and, in point of fact, the force of the letter is conveyed by Lady Macbeth's reaction rather than by the text itself.

'They met me in the day of success, and I have learn'd by the perfect'st report they have more in them than mortal knowledge. When I burn'd in desire to question them further, they made themselves air, into which they vanish'd. Whiles I stood rapt in the wonder of it, came missives from the King, who all-hail'd me Thane of Cawdor, by which title, before, these Weird Sisters saluted me, and referr'd me to the coming on of time with "Hail, King that shalt be!" This have I thought good to deliver thee, my dearest partner of greatness, that thou mightst not lose the dues of rejoicing by being ignorant of what greatness is promis'd thee. Lay it to thy heart, and farewell.' (I, v, 1–15)

The "horrible imaginings" are already working in the mind of Macbeth.

Thanks to Thomas De Quincey, or to its own merit, the Porter's scene (II, iii) has become Shakespeare's most celebrated prose scene. It stands between Duncan's murder and the discovery of the murder, two of the most appalling episodes in a play strong in horrors. It is the perfect illustration of Shakespeare's ability to transform and revitalize a stock device. One expects relaxation, if not "relief," between two such taxing scenes of violence; Shakespeare offers what appears to be that relief, the comic and obscene patter of a drunken clown—but somehow the tension is heightened, not relaxed. The spectators have not been raised from trough to crest to be thrown with greater shock into the next trough. Instead, they realize that the movement has been steadily downward.

The scene opens without transition. Macbeth and Lady Macbeth leave the stage while the knocking is still heard. The Porter enters a moment later, and begins to spin his fantasy without motive or apology. The unseen Macduff has knocked four times before the Porter's appearance, and he knocks half-a-dozen times again before the gate is opened. A pattern of interruption has been created at the end of scene ii, each new barrage of knocks bringing fresh terrors to Macbeth. The Porter, on the other hand, flies into a comic rage against his disturbers, and each time mimics the sound of the knocking. The Porter's choice of hell gate as the scene of his fancied activity is an accurate indication of precisely how amusing this allegedly comic interlude is intended to be. Macbeth, a moment ago, has seen Hell; now the clown pleasantly imagines himself there, and is recalled to his duties only by the cold. His last words before admitting Macduff and Lennox are spoken as much by Shakespeare as by the Porter: "I pray you remember the Porter." The rest of his talk with Macduff is less specifically sinister in its import; it grows naturally out of his intoxication.

The Porter's monologue follows Shakespeare's oldest—
and best—clown-formula, with its personification and ani-
mation of several imaginary characters. The type descends
directly from Launce. In *Macbeth* it is transformed, and
made to deal with strange matter. This is indeed the comedy
of tragedy, for sinister and tragic material is forced into a
familiar comic mold to serve the ends of tragedy.

The short prose dialogue between Lady Macbeth and her
son fulfills a function similar to that of the Porter's scene.
The mother and son are doomed, as Macbeth's last speech
of the preceding scene has indicated. The child's bewilderment is even more poignant than his mother's, because it is
expressed more simply. The timeless and traditional humor
of the child's interrogation of the parent is ironically invoked:

Son. Was my father a traitor, mother?
Wife. Ay, that he was!
Son. What is a traitor?
Wife. Why, one that swears, and lies.
Son. And be all traitors that do so?
Wife. Every one that does so is a traitor and must be hang'd.
Son. And must they all be hang'd that swear and lie?
Wife. Every one.
Son. Who must hang them?
Wife. Why, the honest men.
Son. Then the liars and swearers are fools; for there are liars
and swearers enow to beat the honest men and hang up them.
Wife. Now God help thee, poor monkey! But how wilt thou do
for a father?
Son. If he were dead, you'ld weep for him. If you would not,
it were a good sign that I should quickly have a new father.
Wife. Poor prattler, how thou talk'st! (IV, ii, 44–64)

One may feel that Shakespeare is more or less deliberately
doing violence to the character of the child by making him
speak these last lines; but the total effect of the conversation
remains an overwhelming combination of humor and pathos. Mother and son appear for only a moment; they are

introduced specifically to be murdered. They are simple and normal people, typical of the innocents whom Macbeth is slaughtering. The tragedy of their death is thus generalized to stand for the total effect of Macbeth's cruelty.

Act V is opened by the doctor and gentlewoman whose dialogue supplies the information about Lady Macbeth's affliction, but withholds the essential details that the scene itself reveals. Coming before and after the actual sleepwalking, this discussion frames the scene most effectively; the doctor and gentlewoman's exposition is in prose, perhaps because of the quasi-professional tone of their speeches. After Lady Macbeth has returned to bed, however, the doctor breaks out into an impassioned verse speech, the way for which has been prepared by his interpolated comments during the sleepwalking. The doctor begins by seeking quite specific medical information; what he witnesses both arouses and confirms his suspicions; and he ends by summarizing in verse all the pity and horror he now feels.

The effect of Lady Macbeth's prose is extremely moving. She, who has been seen only as the powerful and determined woman, is now completely shattered; and such is the change that has been wrought in her that she must be presented as unaware of her words and actions, in order that the full extent of her breakdown may be gauged. She and Ophelia are the only tragic heroines who do not speak blank verse in their last appearances on the stage. The pathos of her decline is intensified by her initial overestimation of her own powers. All strength and control have now gone out of her. Shakespeare never made better use of the symbolic representation of mental derangement in prose than in the characterization of Lady Macbeth. Snatches of remembered speech—almost all of them *orders* to Macbeth—are followed by the jingle of "The Thane of Fife had a wife," the whole accompanied by her dreadful hand-washing. The situation in which her derangement is seen contributes greatly to the sense of her complete collapse. For Lady Macbeth exhibits not only the manifestations of insanity, but actually makes her revelations in an unconscious state. The sleep-walking scene may be understood as summing up the whole play. All the themes are reintroduced, all the action recalled, but the conditions under which the recollections are presented demonstrate ironically how far Macbeth and Lady Macbeth are from the days of their greatness.

The compression of *Macbeth* explains why each of the play's prose scenes is almost exemplary of its type. A lost version of the play may have had a highly developed comic plot, but one cannot well conceive it. The few prose scenes are of the utmost dramatic pertinence and make their points with an extraordinary singleness of effect.

11. *Antony and Cleopatra*

Antony and Cleopatra (? 1606–7) bears curious witness to the importance that Shakespeare attached to prose; one might otherwise be at a loss to understand the presence of prose in a play in which everything can be—and is—said so admirably in verse. All the prose is introduced for purely dramatic reasons. None of the chief characters is a "prose speaker"; Enobarbus, who perhaps comes closest to meriting such an appellation, is also the man who speaks the splendid description of Cleopatra's barge (II, ii). If such poetry is assigned to a prose speaker, what may one not expect of the verse speakers!

No more than six scenes involve the use of prose, yet these six offer an extremely rich variety of effect. Act I, scene ii, begins with the teasing of the Soothsayer by Cleopatra's servants. The fact that the Soothsayer's prognostications are in verse makes their seriousness stand out against the mocking prose of Iras and Charmian. The burlesque prayers

to Isis are cut short by Cleopatra's entrance; her irritation
with Antony ("A Roman thought hath struck him") looks
forward to a change of mood in the scene. Her exit, with
Enobarbus and her servants, leaves the stage free to Antony
and his messenger. Their dialogue, and the passage between
Antony and the second messenger, are naturally in verse.
In this mood, Antony is now found by Enobarbus. The ensuing conversation effectively juxtaposes verse and prose;
Enobarbus refuses to take Antony's laconic statements at
all seriously, and each stimulates him to a newer and more
imaginative gibe at Cleopatra. He is brought suddenly to a
dead stop:

> *Antony.* Fulvia is dead.
> *Enobarbus.* Sir?
> *Antony.* Fulvia is dead.
> *Enobarbus.* Fulvia?
> *Antony.* Dead.   (I, ii, 162–166)

But Enobarbus has not been Antony's comrade so long for
nothing, and his cynicism will not permit him to credit this
implausible grief. Eventually only Antony's direct command:
"No more light answers," can make Enobarbus desist. The
use of prose and verse externalizes the conflict between the
two men. Antony is half relieved, half saddened by the news
of Fulvia's death; he is much more moved by the realization
of the grave situation at home, and determines to leave
Cleopatra at once. Enobarbus, unaware of the changed situation in Rome and confident that Antony will be unable to
give Cleopatra up, takes his master's resolution first for one
of a series of unfulfilled decisions to leave, and then as an
expression of purely histrionic grief for Fulvia. Antony
closes the interview with a statement of orders and an explanation of the facts.

Enobarbus' description of Cleopatra has as introduction

a short prose conversation with Agrippa and Mæcenas (II, ii). It is doubly appropriate that the play's most gorgeous speech should be given to the play's most realistic character, and that the speech should emerge suddenly from a discussion of Alexandrian feasts. Enobarbus engages in a more characteristic prose dialogue with Menas, at the end of II, vi; the two men permit themselves an unusual frankness in speaking of their masters' weaknesses and poor judgment. The plainness for which Pompey has praised Enobarbus does not abate when Antony is under consideration.

This scene of candid analysis gives way to an intimate picture of the leaders of the world about their pleasures. They are preceded by servants, who reveal in their prose how far the banquet has progressed. Menas' whispered suggestions of murder to Pompey now play a sinister counterpoint to Antony's baiting of Lepidus in prose. The parallel movement of verse and prose renders admirably the sense of conflicting elements simultaneously at work.

The final scene of *Antony and Cleopatra* introduces the play's most notable prose passage. Cleopatra, forewarned by Dolabella of the rôle she is to play in Cæsar's triumphal journey, sends Charmian to obtain the asps. Charmian's return is followed, a moment later, by the announcement that the fig-seller has arrived, and Cleopatra orders him to be admitted. At this moment, when Cleopatra has at last determined to kill herself, anything in the world may be expected but what Shakespeare actually presents. Cleopatra's death must be like the death of no other Shakespearean heroine; it will very likely entrance the beholder more than it will grieve him. Enobarbus has warned, in quite a different connection, that Cleopatra has an almost sexual delight in feigning death: "I do think there is mettle in death, which commits some loving act upon her, she hath such a celerity in dying." (I, ii, 147-149). And the atmosphere is so

12*

charged with death that Cleopatra's kiss can kill Iras, paining her with pleasure:

> The stroke of death is as a lover's pinch,
> Which hurts, and is desir'd. (V, ii, 298–299)

One nevertheless does not quite expect a clown to be the agent of Cleopatra's death. Not all Cleopatra's farewells will persuade him to leave; she is herself sufficiently intrigued and amused to stimulate him to new efforts with her questions. More than that: she is capable of picking up his line "But I would not be the party that should desire you to touch him, for his biting is immortal," (V, ii, 245–247), and making of it her own exquisite "I have/Immortal longings in me." (V, ii, 283–284).

The Clown's prose creates a not unwelcome suspense, with its ironic comedy, for both Cleopatra and the audience. The queen is a consummate actress who is pleased with the comic interlude, for she can rise from it to the dignified height on which she dies; and it is fitting that the agent of her death should also be the last man to amuse her.

The use of prose in *Antony and Cleopatra* is restricted by the enormously flexible and varied quality of the verse. Except in certain striking instances, such as Enobarbus' baiting of Antony (I, ii), the fluidity of the play makes of verse and prose a single medium, at once infinitely delicate and powerful. But prose is not banished from the play; there are effects which it alone can create. Harley Granville-Barker has well summarized the interaction of prose and verse in *Antony and Cleopatra*: "The freedom and variety of his verse writing allow him to pass almost imperceptibly from poetry to prose and back again. Thus he ranges an unbroken scale, from a pedestrian exactitude in stating plain fact at one end of it to the conventional flourish of the rhymed couplet at the other. But he can still make the sharp contrast of a change effective between scene and scene; or in the midst

of a scene he can bring passion or pretentiousness down to
earth—and prose, or as suddenly restore force and dignity
with rhythm and tone."[61]

12. *Coriolanus*

Prose in Elizabethan drama is paradoxically capable of
expressing the extremes of the rational and irrational. In
such a play as *Hamlet*, the paradox is easily resolved, because it is Hamlet himself who gives voice to both extremes.
A more interesting example, because it more nearly resembles *Coriolanus*, is *Julius Cæsar*, in which prose can serve
both for the mob and for Brutus' futile attempt to convince
the mob on rational grounds. In similar fashion, the two
chief prose speakers in *Coriolanus* are the insensate mob and
the sensible Menenius, sole apostle of reason in an irrational
world.

The first scene of the play deals with one of Menenius'
more successful démarches. Not in the prose which later
becomes so characteristic of him, but in a noble and dignified verse, he calms the mutinous citizens with his fable of
the belly and the members. The Second Citizen, self-appointed spokesman for the plebeians, retorts sarcastically in
prose, but presently urges Menenius on in quite handsome
verse which earns a surprised tribute from the patrician:

> What then?
> Fore me, this fellow speaks! What then? What then?
>
> (I, i, 123—124)

Menenius has almost succeeded in dispersing the mob when
Coriolanus enters to make his first arrogant and contemptuous address to it. The situation is nevertheless settled
for the moment.

The mob in *Julius Cæsar* is shown in various stages of
development as a personality. The mob in *Coriolanus*, at
its first appearance, is the mob of *Julius Cæsar* after Mark

Antony's harangue. It will move from cowardice and irresolution to purposeful action, but its true character is evident from the outset.

A stern lesson in the duties of a hero's wife, in I, iii, becomes, with Valeria's entrance, a pleasing vignette of social life in ancient Rome. The rigorous Volumnia first reproaches her daughter-in-law by recalling her own pride in her warlike boy; when Virgilia asks leave to retire, Volumnia leaves prose for verse and paints a gory picture of Coriolanus in battle. Prose is too tame a medium for her. Valeria's prose conversation adroitly introduces two new facts: the martial temperament of Coriolanus' son and the news of the war. The domestic interlude contributes to an understanding of the psychopathic warrior by illuminating his home life. It is a touch of variety for which one may be thankful; the toga is too often an opaque barrier between the hero and his audience.

Menenius' chat with the tribunes and his joyful meeting with Coriolanus' family are, once again, necessary exposition-scenes skillfully inserted to advance the action without seeming merely utilitarian. The first of the two prose dialogues supplies additional warnings against Brutus and Sicinius at the price of a somewhat garrulous discourse by the "humorous patrician"; the second announces Coriolanus' victorious return and concludes with the curious spectacle of Volumnia and Menenius vying with each other to express their pleasure in the hero's wounds. The entrance of Coriolanus is marked by a change to verse. Brutus and Sicinius remain behind to hatch their plot, and the foreboding of evil in their verse is echoed in the prose of the two officers at the beginning of the following scene. The tribunes rarely speak prose; like the supreme demagogue, Mark Antony, they use verse, the medium of passion, to incite their followers.

The symbolic opposition of prose and verse appears most overtly in II, iii. The knot of citizens, in a prose discussion, agree that Coriolanus deserves their voices. They are friendly enough toward him; the corn question is briefly mentioned, but as quickly forgotten. They see him coming, in the gown of humility, and disperse to return severally. Coriolanus, in a brief verse exchange with Menenius, expresses his disgust at the ceremony forced on him. He then makes the supreme effort, and lowers himself so far as to ask the Citizens, curtly, for their voices. He is franker with the second group, which reproaches him for not loving the common people:

> You should account me the more virtuous that I have not been common in my love. I will, sir, flatter my sworn brother, the people, to earn a dearer estimation of them. 'Tis a condition they account gentle; and since the wisdom of their choice is rather to have my hat than my heart, I will practise the insinuating nod and be off to them most counterfeitly: that is, sir, I will counterfeit the bewitchment of some popular man and give it bountiful to the desirers. Therefore, beseech you I may be consul. (II, iii, 100–110)

He forestalls the third group's questions by addressing them peremptorily in verse, asking six times for "your voices." The custom satisfied, he throws off his prose together with his gown. In Coriolanus' temporary assumption of prose is a touchstone for the difference between the division of verse and prose in this play and the superficially similar one of the earlier Elizabethan drama. In *2 Henry VI* the nobles speak verse and the commons prose primarily because those forms are proper to their respective classes. In *Coriolanus*, it is rather the function of the various characters in the play that determines their use of prose or verse. The haughty Coriolanus can really speak only verse; his prose is once a suggestion of disguise and once an actual disguise. Menenius is a blunt and jovial old man whose informality finds a more felicitous expression in prose than in verse. One is, consequently, not astonished to find him serving as a peacemaker

between the upper and lower classes. The matrons may
speak prose at home, but only verse on the street. Thus there
is a kind of double justification of the verse-prose distribution. The patricians speak verse not because they are patricians but because there is that in their rank (and in their
own awareness of their rank) which makes verse appropriate
to them. In the same way, the plebs speak prose because
prose can best express their confusion and irrationality. The
conflict is a class war, beyond doubt, but the symbolic representation of that war is only superficially paralleled by
the division in the more primitive drama. The Elizabethan
playgoer was accustomed to hear aristocrats speak prose and
plebs and bourgeois speak verse. One cannot, therefore,
merely lump the prose-verse distribution of *Coriolanus* together with that of *Titus Andronicus*.

The exposition-scene of the Roman and Volsce (IV, iii)
does its work simply and rapidly in utilitarian prose. The
names of the two men are introduced because they recognize
each other, but if the plot had not required this detail, the
men would surely have remained as anonymous as the typical
"Gentlemen" or "Citizens" of Shakespeare's exposition-
scenes. The symbolic force of the union of former enemies,
even though the question of their personal identity is of no
importance, prepares the audience for the far more dramatic
union of Coriolanus and Aufidius.

Coriolanus' prose disguise in II, iii, is as transparent as
his donning of the gown of humility is contemptuous; but
the long scene in Aufidius' house in Antium (IV, v) sees the
fallen hero in a double and literal disguise. His tattered
clothes make the servants take him for a vagabond and address him as such. Coriolanus retorts in prose of equal rough-
ness, after making one vain attempt to control his temper.
When Aufidius questions him, he replies in verse, as an equal.
The exit of the two generals leaves the scene to the two serv-

ants, who comment in prose on what they have witnessed.
The third servant comes in to describe Coriolanus' reception
by the Volscian nobles. The scene is allowed to end on a
comic note of nationalism. The satirical point of this deliberately vulgarized conclusion seems plain enough: the Vol-
scians will prove as untrustworthy and ungrateful as the Romans, and Coriolanus will be thwarted in his plan of revenge.
These representatives of another mob first threaten and then
fawn on Coriolanus, praising themselves for having discern-
ed the hero's true nobility through his disguise. They are
as fickle as their brothers in Rome, who at this moment are
berating each other for having banished Coriolanus.

Menenius, at last persuaded that he should intercede, goes
to see Coriolanus in the Volscian camp (V, ii). He argues
civilly in verse with the obdurate guards; as they grow more
heated, they pass to prose. Menenius then accosts Coriolanus in his humorous, wordy prose, trying to reëstablish the
atmosphere of friendliness and intimacy which existed previously between them. Coriolanus rebuffs him in a cruel
verse, gives him a letter, and leaves, not forgetting to point
out his own severity to Aufidius. The guard's gibes sting
Menenius, whose weary bitterness is perhaps the best measure of his shock and disappointment. His earlier style
reappears in his description of Coriolanus' fierce determination (V, iv). The mood of the scene lifts at the second messenger's report of peace, and Menenius acclaims Volumnia
in verse.

There remains one fragment of prose in the play. It is the
disorganized shout of the Volscian people:

Tear him to pieces! — Do it presently! — He kill'd my son! — My
daughter! — He kill'd my cousin Marcus! — He kill'd my father!
(V, vi, 120–123)

This mob five minutes earlier has cheered Coriolanus'
entrance into Corioles; it now cries for his blood, and the

echo of this cry is in the twice-banished hero's ears as the conspirators stab him. The acceptance of the mob's speedy change of heart involves one in no great effort of the imagination. The mob's fickleness is a phenomenon which Shakespeare never takes great pains to render plausible, perhaps because he was confident of his audience's prompt and understanding response. In *Julius Cæsar* he strained plausibility somewhat more, causing the mob to change sides twice in as brief a space of time.

The subject of *Coriolanus*, the war between a proud man and the people for whom he has an unnatural hatred puts to advantage the conflict between prose and verse. The opposition, like the import of the whole play, is not unambiguous. Coriolanus gives voice to his unreason in verse, the people in prose. Menenius, an interested commentator unable to give free rein to his satirical mind, advocates in humorous garrulity a policy of moderation. If Shakespeare had had no *parti pris* (but one must suspect he had), Menenius might have taken his place in the gallery of satirical prose commentators.

In Shakespeare's tragedies appears the fullest and richest expression of his use of prose for dramatic contrast. The comedies have a more direct claim on prose as their proper medium, whereas the prose of tragedy must justify its presence by providing a contrast which heightens and intensifies the tragic effect.

Shakespeare's technique, unlike that of his fellow-dramatists, underwent a systematic development as he extended and elaborated the prose convention. Some of his contemporaries and successors paralleled various stages of this development and borrowed what they found useful. But Shakespeare stands alone in the imaginative variety of his technique.

Shakespeare generally employed the prose convention to produce dramatic contrast; at least once, however, in *King Lear*, he achieved with its aid an effect of synthesis or harmony. In the same play, however, he continued to employ the convention for effects of contrast, giving it new and rich expression. In *Julius Cæsar*, and, still more effectively, in *Hamlet*, prose is used for denigration, reduction, and satire. Iago's prose in *Othello* is almost a classic example of this technique in action. The prose of denigration was Shakespeare's single greatest development of the prose convention, and was most successfully imitated by such men as Webster, Tourneur, and Ford.

The breakdown of blank verse and the consequent blurring of distinction between verse and prose perhaps manifests itself in *Timon of Athens*, certainly in *King Lear*. But Shakespeare continues to respect the convention, even when using it for synthesis as well as for antithesis. He was capable of transforming the use to which he put the convention, but not of dispensing with prose altogether.

VI

Conclusion

Behind Shakespeare's use of prose lies the history of the prose convention in the Elizabethan drama. The term is ambiguous, for no single convention governed the use of prose in the English drama at the beginning of Shakespeare's career. There were, instead, several conventional uses of prose which were apparently unconnected: prose was used for letters and proclamations, for the representation of madness, and for comic matter. None of Shakespeare's predecessors seems to have been aware of a dramatic principle unifying these uses; and virtually the same eclecticism characterized the work even of some of Shakespeare's contemporaries and successors.

The origins of those first conventional uses remain more or less obscure. Definite proof is lacking, but in all likelihood common experience furnished the idea for letter- and proclamation-prose. The well-known elaborate and heavy prose of the typical proclamation, for example, made it impossible for a dramatist to present verse proclamations on the stage. One cannot tell how or when empirical information combined with a developing sense of dramatic decorum to produce a convention.

Mad prose offers a similar problem. The figuring of insanity by some sort of incoherent speech or babbling satisfied the Elizabethan playgoer, whether or not he had first-hand experience of mad speech. At some point in the development of this usage, it became understood that the speech of the lunatic was prose, and not broken verse. Thus usage was transformed into convention.

The use of prose for comic matter appears to have grown out of doggerel or "tumbling verse,"[62] which was confused with—and eventually became—prose. A sense of the realistic nature of comic action doubtless contributed to the ready acceptance of this use of prose. Closely allied to comic prose was the more general use of prose for low characters. In speaking of the early drama, one may appear to be drawing a distinction without a difference, since most of the low characters are comedians; but the independent development of comic prose and prose for people of lower social classes indicates that the divergence goes back to an earlier differentiation.

Lyly was the first Elizabethan dramatist to use prose intelligently and effectively. The all-prose play was a form in which he could successfully exploit the rhetorical devices which had made him famous, but he soon found it necessary to transform Euphuism quite drastically in order to use it in dramatic prose. His plays, studied chronologically, show a steady decline in the employment of Euphuistic figures. (His one verse play, *The Woman in the Moone*, obeys the conventions of mad prose and comic prose.) Lyly's pioneering work in dramatic prose influenced Shakespeare and other dramatists, but only Jonson and Chapman followed him in writing all-prose plays.

Kyd, Marlowe, Peele and Greene all used prose with varying degrees of sophistication and success. Zabina's mad prose in *Tamburlaine, Part I*, must have impressed Shakespeare by its artful use of repetition and its dramatic appositeness. In the main, however, the tendency of the pre-Shakespearean drama was to observe the conventional uses of prose and to make a rough division of prose for comic and verse for serious matter. Contrast was, of course, implicit in this division; nevertheless, a playwright whose comic plot had little or no relation to his serious plot must have thought that, by putting one plot in prose and the other in verse, he was separating the two actions rather than contrasting them. When prose and verse characters appeared in the same scene, the principle of contrast obviously dominated the division.

Shakespeare's plays show, almost from the beginning, the use of prose for dramatic contrast. So early a play as *Romeo and Juliet* strongly opposes the regular verse of the romantic tragic action to the prose of both high and low comic action. Prose quickly established itself in Shakespeare's work as a vital form for comedy. Its realistic quality was exploited to splendid effect in such plays as *Henry IV*, *As You Like It*, and *Twelfth Night*. It is possible to say that, by the middle of his career, Shakespeare had woven the various conventional usages into a single prose convention, whose basic principle was to offer dramatic contrast with verse, and whose potentialities he was to explore more and more fully. His development of the use of prose for comic and realistic effect is reflected in the works of Dekker and Beaumont and Fletcher, as may be seen in such plays as *The Shoemaker's Holiday*, *The Honest Whore*, and *The Knight of the Burning Pestle*.

The course of the convention's development in Shakespeare's comedies is not quite parallel to that in his tragedies. The contrast between the comic and the serious plots in *Much Ado About Nothing* is one between comic realistic action and romantic action; broadly speaking, a similar contrast is found in many of the comedies. But Shakespeare discovered that tragedy offered far more fertile ground for experiments in contrast. In *Hamlet* he employed prose as no one had done before, save for his own experiment with prose of satire, denigration, and reduction in Casca's account of Cæsar's rejection of the crown. Any given thing, honor, virtue, the world itself, can be made to seem great in verse; it can be diminished and cheapened in prose.

Shakespeare used this new technique with great effect in *Troilus and Cressida* for the character of Thersites, whose railing produces a systematic reduction of the Greek heroes. (Heywood's Thersites in *The Iron Age* parallels him in dramatic function and in the use of prose.) Iago exemplifies the same intent; *Othello* is a study of his application of this technique to bring about catastrophe. The satirical commentator and the villain illustrate perfectly Shakespeare's application of his most important and imaginative extension of the prose convention.

Various playwrights followed Shakespeare in this new use of prose. Marston's *The Malcontent* and Middleton and Rowley's *The Changeling* show clear traces of Shakespeare's influence; in the work of Webster is the finest expression, outside Shakespeare, of reduction and denigration through prose. It is this conception that informs the whole character of Flamineo and, to a lesser extent, that of Bosola. Tourneur and Ford, under the influence of this new aspect of the prose convention, created, respectively, Vendice and D'Avolos.

The growing irregularity of blank verse in the Jacobean drama, and the consequent blurring of distinction between prose and verse, contributed to the weakening of the prose convention by attacking the very structural basis of the prose-verse drama. Webster, who had a fine sense of the distinction of forms, nevertheless did not hesitate to mingle blank verse, prose, and couplets in a single speech; he also violated the prose convention, by using verse in the mad scenes of Brachiano and Cornelia, when he thought the total dramatic effect would gain by it. The colloquial quality of Fletcher's verse, which is caused by its irregularity, may help to explain the elimination of prose from his later plays.

The decline in regularity of Shakespeare's verse may be associated, in such a play as *King Lear*, with a transcendence of the prose convention. The principle of contrast governs the distribution of prose and verse during the greater part of the convention's history. Now, however, the mixture of prose, blank verse, and song in the farmhouse-scene in *King Lear* is employed to produce an effect of harmonious blending and synthesis. But Shakespeare at the same time uses the principle of contrast in *King Lear*, when he opposes the prose-scenes dominated by Edmund (another example of the use of prose for reduction) to the verse-scenes of the principal plot. Contrast, rather than synthesis, explains Shakespeare's division of prose and verse.

The decline of blank verse helped prepare the way for the emergence of prose as the form for the drama. Many factors and tendencies, naturally, combined to bring about the change in form: a growing realism, a dominant interest in comedy, and a dearth of great dramatic poets. The heroic play had prose for its comic parts, and, on the other side, so realistic a comedy as *The Plain Dealer* had verse soliloquies. But this self-conscious imitation of earlier models could not keep alive the prose-verse play.

When one attempts to set Shakespeare against the background of his contemporaries and successors in order to arrive at a more precise idea of his achievement in the prose convention, one is driven to the conclusion that his practice was unparalleled. With only the simplest conventional uses of prose to guide him, and with the example of Lyly's all-prose plays, which gave few or no hints for the prose-verse play, Shakespeare developed prose into a subtle, sensitive medium. Comedy and tragedy profited equally by his extension of the convention; the greatly elaborated use of prose for realistic effect and the sardonic, cynical prose of Hamlet both inspired admiration and imitation among Shakespeare's colleagues. But none of them had the imagination or audacity to attempt all his uses of the convention. Aspects of his work in prose are reflected in plays by other men; but the entire conception of underlying contrast, with all its ramifications, is his alone.

Shakespeare's development in the use of prose is almost entirely independent. Comparison between his work and the contemporary drama reveals some parallels, but any attempt to relate his technique consistently to that of any other Elizabethan or Jacobean dramatist is doomed to failure. The study of Shakespeare's work against the background of the dramatic literature of his time emphasizes the uniqueness of his achievements. Many of his contemporaries used prose in a haphazard fashion according to the exigencies of the individual play; Shakespeare was not exempt from these concerns or from the demands of popular taste, but he constructed his work according to a consistent principle that supplemented and strengthened the structure and movement of each play. That principle could be transcended; Shakespeare wrote at least one part of *King Lear* in a medium formed of both prose and verse in a strange and new combination. Throughout Shakespeare's work, one is conscious of plan and order, of a deliberate and sensitive choice of forms. His technique was not conceived theoretically and applied uncompromisingly, but was developed out of sound observation in the theatre.

Another feature of Shakespeare's prose that makes it preëminent is its beauty and variety as literary prose. He cannot ever have considered prose a medium inferior to verse, for he never allowed such a prejudice to color his work, as did many of his contemporaries. Heywood, for example, appears to have viewed prose as a necessary but contemptible form, good enough for clownish servants and rough louts, but rarely worthy of greater figures. Who can read *Hamlet*, on the other hand, without feeling that Shakespeare is concerned to make his prose as beautiful as his verse? There are undistinguished passages of prose in his plays, it must be admitted, where utilitarian considerations have the upper hand; but there are equally pedestrian passages of verse.

The excellence of Shakespeare's prose consists in its simplicity, ease, and naturalness, and in the care and subtlety with which the differentiation of prose styles is made to contribute to the creation of character. J. H. Francis has admirably summarized these qualities of the prose: "Shakespeare wrote as the musician composes, hearing the actual sound of his instrument, in this case, the human voice . . . On the stage, where no two characters should think or speak alike, the dramatist requires—at least as a theoretical ideal—as many styles as there are characters. How closely Shakespeare approached this ideal can be appreciated by comparing his dialogue with that of Ben Jonson, in whose plays so many characters talk alike that we must assume that they all talked like Ben Jonson."[63] One need only compare the prose of Benedick and Rosalind to see how artfully Shakespeare differentiates the prose styles of speakers who are not very different in temperament. The chief characteristic of both styles is mocking humor; but the masculinity of Benedick's style, with its short periods "huddling jest upon jest" and demolishing the opponent with the swiftness of their repeated blows, is in sharp contrast to the slower and more circumstantial style of Rosalind. Benedick's account of his meeting with Beatrice is spoken at high speed and in a burlesque fury; Rosalind's disquisition on lovedeaths (how happily different from Wagner's *Liebestod!*) states its conclusion first, then slowly and with deliberate sarcasm presents its examples, nails them down—"But these are all lies"—and concludes in mock-logical fashion: "Men have died from time to time, and worms have eaten them, but not for love." The style, compared with Benedick's, is feminine. Benedick returns again and again to the attack, stopping momentarily to calm himself—"Come, talk not of her" —only promptly to disobey his own injunction. Rosalind's shafts are fewer but no less destructive; her style is slow and insinuating, obtaining its effect by a series of long and short periods: "Leander, he would have liv'd many a fair year though Hero had turn'd nun, if it had not been for a hot midsummer night; for (good youth) he went but forth to wash him in the Hellespont, and being taken with the cramp, was drown'd; and the foolish chroniclers of that age found it was 'Hero of Sestos.' " Benedick, of the two, has the sharper tongue; but Rosalind has the better wit. Benedick's is a humor of extremes, and he is consequently capable of being involuntarily funny; Rosalind insists on reducing legend to fact, with a humor rooted in a common-sense view of the world. These differences in the nature of their humor are mirrored in the rhythmic and logical texture of their prose styles.

The fact that one can speak of Shakespeare's prose styles prejudges the question of whether he has a single prose style. Various characters have appropriate styles, which have certain characteristics in common, such as colloquialness, vigor, and simplicity. Tempo, on the other hand, is a variable; length of period is another. Repetition produces one effect in Hamlet's advice to the players, and quite a different one in Falstaff's speech, which Mark Van Doren has brilliantly defined: "(Falstaff) is limited as a mimic only by the facts of his physique; being old and fat, he is short of breath and so must be brief of phrase ... But it will be seen at once —or heard—that he has made the most of this limitation. Artist that he is, he has accepted its challenge and employed it in effects that express his genius with a notable and economical directness. If he must gasp he will make each further gasp an echo of its fellow—an echo, but with ineffable additions. His speech then is not merely brief; it is repetitive, it rolls back on itself, it picks up its theme and tosses it to us again, with rich improvements."[64]

Shakespeare's prose is always *dramatic* prose; its effects are conceived in terms of the listening spectator. Shakespeare uses prose for dramatic contrast with verse, and thus makes conflict, which is at the basis of all drama, command the very language of his plays.

APPENDIX I

A Note on the Printing of Prose and Verse in Shakespeare

It may appear to some that a fundamental problem has been ignored in this study. Have not the decisions of the editors concerning the printing of prose and verse in Shakespeare's plays been accepted too unquestioningly? Generally speaking, there is really no problem, for Shakespeare's prose and verse are ordinarily easily distinguished; and the editors have almost always been quite correct in emending the printers' most obvious mistakes.

At this point, we may do well to examine some of these errors. They are extremely numerous, as may be seen from the following list of variations for *Romeo and Juliet*, *Hamlet*, and *1 Henry IV*. The texts compared are: for *Romeo and Juliet*, Q1, Q2, Q3, and F; for *Hamlet*, Q1, Q2, Q4, and F; and for *1 Henry IV*, Q1, Q5, Q6, and F. The modern text used as a control is the Cambridge edition, ed. W. A. Neilson (Boston, 1906).

Romeo and Juliet

Q1. Verse printed as prose:
    I, iii, 71–76.
    I, v, 114–118, 143–146.
    II, i, 7–21, 23–29.
    II, v, 64–66.
    IV, v, 1–16.
    V, i, 77–79.
    Total: 49 lines.
    Prose printed as verse:
    IV, v, 128–131.
    Total: 4 lines.

Q2. Verse printed as prose:
     I, iv, 54–91.
     II, iv, 1, 2.
     III, i, 3, 4.
     IV, v, 102.
     Total: 43 lines.
     Prose printed as verse:
     III, i, 40, 41.
     IV, v, 141–144.
     Total: 6 lines.

Q3. Verse printed as prose:
     I, iii, 2, 3, 4–48, 50–57, 59–62, 67, 68.
     I, iv, 54–91.
     II, iv, 1, 2.
     Total: 104 lines.

F. Verse printed as prose:
     I, iii, 7–12, 16–62, 67, 68, 75, 76.
     I, iv, 53–91.
     Total: 95 lines.
     Prose printed as verse:
     IV, v, 102–119, 124–127, 141–144.
     Total: 26 lines.

Hamlet

Q1. Verse printed as prose:
     II, ii, 160, 161.
     IV, iv, 20–22.
     Total: 5 lines.

Q2. Verse printed as prose:
     II, ii, 181–227, 280–474.
     III, ii, 53–55.
     Total: 254 lines.
     Prose printed as verse:
     IV, iii, 40, 41, 50–55.
     IV, iv, 33, 34, 36, 56–58, 67, 170–174.
     Total: 20 lines.

Q4. Verse printed as prose:
    III, ii, 53–55.
    Total: 3 lines.
    Prose printed as verse:
    III, i, 155–157.
    III, ii, 97–104.
    Total: 11 lines.
 F. Verse printed as prose:
    IV, v, 168, 169, 187–189.
    Total: 5 lines.
    Prose printed as verse:
    II, ii, 207–218.
    Total: 12 lines.

1 Henry IV

Q1. Verse printed as prose:
    II, ii, 111–118.
    II, iii, 73–91.
    II, iv, 555–560.
    III, i, 3–10, 107–111.
    Total: 46 lines.
    Prose printed as verse:
    III, i, 229–239.
    V, i, 121–124.
    V, iii, 49, 50.
    Total: 17 lines.
Q5. Verse printed as prose:
    II, ii, 111–118.
    II, iii, 73–91.
    II, iv, 555–560.
    IV, ii, 82–86.
    Total: 38 lines.
    Prose printed as verse:
    III, i, 229–239.
    III, iii, 216, 217.
    V, i, 121–124.
    V, iii, 49, 50.
    Total: 19 lines.

Q6. Shows same errors as Q5.

  F. Verse printed as prose:

    II, ii, 111–115.
    II, iii, 73–91.
    II, iv, 555–560.
    IV, ii, 82–86.
    V, iii, 132, 133.
    Total: 37 lines.

    Prose printed as verse:

    III, i, 198–200, 236–239, 250–255.
    III, iii, 192–200, 216, 217.
    V, i, 121–124.
    Total: 28 lines.

These variations are at least curious. At one time, it seemed conceivable to the writer that the Elizabethan printers could serve as rough guides to the Elizabethan conception of a verse-prose division. With greater experience of the ways of those printers came the sad realization that they could hardly be used as trustworthy guides to anything.

Consider the list of variations in *Romeo and Juliet*. Some are insignificant, but two are not: the Nurse's speech (I, iii, 16–62) and Mercutio's speech (I, iv, 53–91). Both the Nurse and Mercutio speak prose and verse in the play, although they are characters who, in a later play, would probably speak only prose. Shakespeare is just beginning to develop and unify the prose convention. The Nurse's speech appears as prose in Q3 and F, and Mercutio's speech is so printed in Q2, Q3, and F. Obviously one need not at once explain away these errors by suggesting that the printers responsible obeyed their highly-developed literary instincts and set up the speeches in what seemed to them the proper form, against the bidding of their copy. J. Dover Wilson offers a final statement about that copy: "If there is one lesson to be learnt from a bibliographical study of the Good Quartos, it is that the compositors had no means of distinguishing between prose and verse except by line-division in their copy."[65]

There are other and more practical explanations of misprinting by the compositor. Sir E. K. Chambers cites three instances in which verse has been spaced out as prose by the compositor to fill out a page, where matters had gone too far to permit resetting of the entire page.[66] Professor W. A. Jackson of Harvard University has suggested a similar general principle to explain grosser errors of this sort. When the compositor owned his own shop, he was often tempted to print verse as prose in order to save paper; when, on the other hand, he was an employee paid according to the number of pages composed, he might print prose as verse in order to earn more money.

Where any and all indications to the printer presumably were lacking, as in the "Bad Quarto" of *Hamlet*, the play has been set up almost entirely in a kind of botched blank verse. This instance, with many others, reminds us that we frequently cannot depend even on the physical appearance of the page in the Quarto or Folio to tell us whether we are dealing with verse or prose. Both margins are irregular and inconclusive. The consideration of economy has even caused non-dramatic verse to be printed as prose.

Again, a scene printed as prose in one edition may have been reset as verse in a later edition to give a false semblance of reworking or reëditing. This is, of course, pure conjecture; the Elizabethans purchased the latest edition of a play to have the latest edition, not to compare it with earlier editions.

One can only wonder whether the typesetter of the First Folio, or of the *Romeo and Juliet* quartos, was at all aware of the patent absurdity of printing as prose speeches which are so obviously in verse. The modern reader, armed with well-edited texts, can only with difficulty recapture the state of mind of that printer whom Professor Kittredge damned as the most unreliable of human beings. We can never know conclusively whether complete insensitivity, stupidity, or ulterior purpose governed his ridiculous mistakes.

In the main, then, it seems impossible to draw any large conclusions from the misprinting of prose as verse and vice versa. Our information is too scanty; the printer, that all-important unknown on whom we should have to base the greatest portion of our case, is not to be trusted; and there are, beyond question, many variables of which sufficient knowledge cannot be obtained.

A Note on the Text of 'As You Like It'

It is taken for granted in this study that we are dealing with the prose-verse division as it is found in the latest and most authoritative editions of Shakespeare's plays, rather than with the state of the text at some earlier stage in the composition of any or all of the plays. If it were possible to produce an earlier version of a play which would show (as does the Italianate version of Jonson's *Every Man in his Humour*) verse scenes later reworked in prose, or vice versa, one might discover invaluable information concerning Shakespeare's dramaturgic technique. But, unfortunately, no such information exists. It is tempting to regard the hastily-contrived prose scenes in *Timon of Athens* as scenes only sketched out in prose, but there is no evidence. If we assume that Shakespeare's plays as we have them represent the most nearly complete state of those plays which we can hope to have, we must not regard them as working manuscripts, and we must refrain from juggling with the text to produce attractive but unverifiable "earlier stages" of composition.

There would be no cause to advance such strictures if experiments of this sort had not already been made. Among them, the most complete and perhaps most unreliable is that of J. Dover Wilson,[67] who has applied himself to the Folio text of *As You Like It* with truly astonishing results. He states that an earlier version of *As You Like It*, in verse, underlies our text: "History of a kind lies behind the transmitted text, since it is evident that some of the scenes now in prose had once been in blank verse. The textual editor owes the discovery of this fact to Dr. A. W. Pollard, who when making a study of *As You Like It* some years ago, came to the conclusion that the prose-lines with which 5.2 opens had originally been verse ..."[68]

These are the lines:

Orlando. Is't possible that on so little acquaintance you should like her? that but seeing you should love her? and loving woo? and wooing, she should grant? And will you persever to enjoy her?

Oliver. Neither call the giddiness of it in question, the poverty of her, the small acquaintance, my sudden wooing, nor her sudden consenting; but say with me, I love Aliena; say with her that she loves me; consent with both that we may enjoy each other. It shall be to your good; for my father's house and all the revenue that was old Sir Rowland's, will I estate upon you, and here live and die a shepherd.

Orlando. You have my consent. Let your wedding be tomorrow. Thither will I invite the duke and all's contented followers. Go you and prepare Aliena; for look you, here comes my Rosalind. (V, ii, 1–19)

Wilson would have us believe that these prose speeches represent a later development of Shakespeare's original verse draft. And he attempts to prove this contention by recasting the passage in verse: "If two small words be omitted," he says, ten of the first eighteen lines of the scene "form a continuous passage which even the most sceptical or the most conservative of critics must admit to be verse."[69] For the sake of argument, let us admit his altered reading to be verse. But if, by any effort of the imagination, his verse could be assumed to be identical with Shakespeare's first effort, then the poet indeed did well to change it to prose. Wilson uncovers these "verse fossils" (the term is his):

> Consent with both that we (may) enjoy each other:
> It shall be to your good; (for) my father's house
> And all the revenue that was old Sir Rowland's
> Will I estate upon you, and here live
> And die a shepherd.

Orlando.   You have my consent...
Let your wedding be to-morrow: thither will I
Invite the duke and all's contented followers:
Go you and prepare Aliena; for look you,
Here comes my Rosalind.[70]

We may with reason be suspicious of the "slight changes" which are necessary to transform the passage into verse. For further "verse fossils" are uncovered in the earlier lines of the scene, again necessitating "a little alteration."

> Is't possible that on so *slight* acquaintance
>
> But seeing you should love (her)? and loving woo?
> And wooing she should grant? (and) will you
>   perséver
>
> My sudden wooing nor her *quick* consenting;
> But say with me, I love *my* Aliena.[71]

By now, Wilson is doing more than merely dropping out a word to make a pentameter line. The recesses of the creative imagination are plumbed for the original poetic word that makes verse out of crass prose.

The rest of the argument is based on prose passages in three scenes: I, ii; II, vi; and IV, iii. In the first, Wilson reaps a rich harvest of verse fossils with the aid of what he calls, with unwonted candor, "a little innocent faking." Why is it necessary to assume an earlier verse-form for this portion of the wrestling-scene, which contrasts effectively with the romantic episode which closes the scene? Shakespeare's other plays of the same period habitually cast such matter in prose.

The second passage shows a scene (II, vi) which is printed as verse in the Folio and is given by Quiller-Couch and Wilson as the prose it clearly is. Wilson nevertheless remains convinced that the hypothetical original had a verse scene, and his "innocent faking" yields us yet another treasure-trove of verse fossils:

> No greater heart in thee? Live *yet* a little,
> Comfort a little, cheer thyself a little.
> If this *wild* forest *any thing savage yield.*[72]

as against

> Live a little, comfort a little, cheer thyself a little. If this un-
> couth forest yield any thing savage... (II, vi, 5–6)

Poets may make good editors, but the reverse is not necessarily true.

The third passage (IV, iii) involves Wilson in the rather complicated assumption that the half-lines of prose which convert the entire passage into prose represent longer verse-passages cut down. Again, the Folio prints the lines as verse, against the evidence of the senses.

Even if one obediently swallows Wilson's whale, it is more than a gnat at which he asks one to strain in his comments on the Jaques-Rosalind dialogue in IV, i. He converts Jaques' speech on his melancholy (ll. 10–19) into verse, changing only the words "By my faith" to "'i' faith," but completely gives himself away in his comment on the line "Nay then, God b' wi' you, an you talk in blank verse":

> Jaques' gibe at blank verse (1. 29) makes it quite certain, of course,
> that Shakespeare deliberately converted the verse into prose.[73]

What is one to understand by this? If Shakespeare wrote the scene originally in verse, Jaques' line would be meaningless. In the received text, Orlando's greeting, "Good day, and happiness, dear Rosalind!" (l. 28) comes as a striking verse interruption in the prose dialogue and gives point to Jaques' gibe, whereas, if verse had been the medium of the conversation, Orlando's verse would have created no disturbing element and excited no comment. And why should Shakespeare introduce so ambiguous a backward glance at his own hypothetical first version? Jaques' remark proves that the foregoing dialogue is in prose, and hits at Orlando for his stiltedness, which contrasts with the freedom and movement of the preceding speeches.

In his notes on the copy of *The Tempest*,[74] *The Two Gen-tlemen of Verona*,[75] and *Measure for Measure*[76] appended to the Cambridge edition of those plays as edited by himself and Quiller-Couch, Wilson pursues the same line of attack, although not with the completeness of his essay on *As You Like It*. The technique, in its essentials, is the same; one elaboration should, however, be noted: the rewriting of verse scenes in prose in *The Two Gentlemen of Verona* is ascribed to some hand other than Shakespeare's. The object of the revision in these three plays is, according to the editor, to shorten the reviser's received text, whether or not that reviser was Shakespeare. And it is undoubtedly true that such telescoping of scenes as Wilson describes could more easily be managed in prose than in verse, although the evidence presented may not establish that this play is an illustration of the process.

Wilson's study of *As You Like It* displays the characteristic virtuosity and the weakness of his scholarship; he is ingenious to a fault, but he entirely fails to supply any adequate motive for the transformations he detects. He at no time makes clear the conclusion which his boneyard of verse fossils is intended to support. Although he is satisfied that he knows the nature of the verse scenes which underlie the prose scenes, he seems unaware of any formal or dramatic difference between the hypothetical earlier versions and the received text. In terms of criticism, his case is thereby greatly weakened. Shakespeare is too accomplished a dramatist to transform an *As You Like It* so radically without apparent motive; and Wilson, who is so gifted a discerner of the author's intention, leaves this question unanswered.

The entire hypothesis of the "verse fossil" is not above suspicion. The iamb is notoriously one of the commonest rhythms in English speech; The New York *Times* will yield as many verse fossils as Shakespeare's prose. Pentameter is a normal enough rhetorical period in ordinary speech or writing. In a conversation on Wilson's theory, the late Professor Kittredge analyzed a fragment of the discussion and harvested three iambic pentameter verse fossils in as many sentences.

If it is possible to obtain such results from the speech of men who are not poets, what may one not expect to find in Shakespeare's prose? About two-fifths of Shakespeare's entire text is in prose. But the playwright was after all a poet; and it would indeed be extraordinary if some verse effects and verse lines did not crop up in his prose.

If one were to adopt Wilson's theory, what might one expect to learn about Shakespeare's technique of composition? Only enough, it must be feared, to make one think that his technique differed profoundly from that of most other playwrights; and that statement is no contribution to Shakespeare-idolatry. William Drummond of Hawthornden says of Ben Jonson "That he wrote all his [verses] first in prose, for so his master, Camden, had learned him." [77] It is difficult to know whether "verses" should be understood to include Jonson's plays and, if so, whether Jonson's method was sufficiently typical to tell us anything about Shakespeare's practice. Once the initial difficulty is overcome, however, the second point seems not impossible. Racine is known to have written his plays first in prose; there is good reason to suppose that Molière did the same, and that some non-dramatic poets, including Virgil, wrote first drafts in prose. Prose to verse appears by far a more logical progression than verse to prose, and we should probably be safe in assuming that a first draft of a play would more reasonably be written in prose than in verse . . . if we need follow Wilson in indulging such fantasies. It seems an unrewarding exercise of the imagination.

ACKNOWLEDGMENTS

For permission to quote from their publications, the author's thanks are due to F. L. Lucas, for passages from his edition of the plays of John Webster; to Henry W. Wells, for a passage from his essay, "The Continuity of Shaksperian Prose"; and to the following publishers:

To the Cambridge University Press, for passages from Richard David's *The Janus of Poets*, from J. Dover Wilson's *The Manuscript of Shakespeare's Hamlet*, and from the following volumes of *The New Shakespeare*, edited by Arthur Quiller-Couch and J. Dover Wilson: *As You Like It*, *The Tempest*, *The Two Gentlemen of Verona*, and *Measure for Measure*.

To Chatto and Windus, Ltd., for a passage from C. E. Montague's "Shakspere's Way With Agincourt," published in *Dramatic Values*.

To Ginn and Company, for passages from George Lyman Kittredge's edition of *The Complete Works of Shakespeare*.

To Harcourt, Brace and Company, and to Messrs. Christy and Moore, Ltd., for a passage from George Orwell's "The Art of Donald McGill," published in *Dickens, Dali and Others*.

To the Hogarth Press, for material from George H. W. Rylands' *Words and Poetry*.

To Henry Holt and Company, for passages from Mark Van Doren's *Shakespeare*.

To the Oxford University Press, for passages from E. K. Chambers' *William Shakespeare*, R. W. Bond's edition of *The Works of John Lyly*, C. F. Tucker Brooke's edition of *The Works of Christopher Marlowe*, F. S. Boas' edition of *The Works of Thomas Kyd*, and the C. H. Herford-Percy Simpson edition of *The Works of Ben Jonson*.

To the Princeton University Press, for passages from Harley Granville-Barker's *Prefaces to Shakespeare*.

NOTES

1. *Words and Poetry* (London, 1928), Part II, *passim*.
2. "The Prose in Shakspere's Plays," *Transactions of the New Shakspere Society* (London, 1880–86), p. 558.
3. R. Warwick Bond, *The Works of John Lyly* (Oxford, 1902), II, 287.
4. *Ibid.*, 289.
5. *Ibid.*, II, 464–466.
6. *Ibid.*, II, 466.
7. *Ibid.*, III, 282.
8. *Ibid.*
9. *Ibid.*, II, 296.
10. *The Works of Christopher Marlowe*, ed. C. F. Tucker Brooke (Oxford, 1910), pp. 64–65.
11. *Ibid.*, p. 7.
12. *Ibid.*, pp. 163–4.
13. *The Tragical History of Dr. Faustus*, ed. F. S. Boas, (London, 1932), Introduction, pp. 26–32.
14. Brooke, *op. cit.*, p. 141.
15. *Ibid.*, p. 287.
16. *The Works of Thomas Kyd*, ed. F. S. Boas (Oxford, 1901), p. 67.
17. *Ibid.*, p. 69.
18. *Ibid.*, pp. 67, 68.
19. *Ibid.*, p. 68.
20. *The Works of George Peele*, ed. A. H. Bullen (London, 1888), I, 334.
21. Richard David, *The Janus of Poets* (London, 1935), p. 8.
22. J. F. Macdonald, "The Use of Prose in English Drama Before Shakespeare," *University of Toronto Quarterly*, II, 4 (Toronto, July, 1933), 480.
23. Henry W. Wells, "The Continuity of Shaksperian Prose," *Shakespeare Association Bulletin*, XV, 3 (July, 1940), 175–183.
24. *Ben Jonson*, ed. C. H. Herford and Percy Simpson, Vol. V (London, 1937), 56, 57.
25. *The Works of Ben Jonson*, ed. Brinsley Nicholson and C. H. Herford (London, 1893–95), I, Introduction, xvii.

26. *Ben Jonson*, ed. Herford and Simpson, III (London, 1927), 479.

27. *Ibid.*, IV (London, 1932), 74.

28. *The Best Plays of Beaumont and Fletcher*, ed. J. St. Loe Strachey (London, 1887), I, 11.

29. *Ibid.*, pp. 96, 97.

30. *Ibid.*, p. 97.

31. *Ibid.*, p. 132.

32. *Ibid.*, p. 120.

33. *Ibid.*, p. 126.

34. *Ibid.*, II, 330.

35. *Ibid.*, II, 392.

36. *Ibid.*, II, 396, 397.

37. Thomas Dekker, *Selected Plays*, ed. Ernest Rhys (London, 1894), p. 73.

38. *The Complete Works of John Webster*, ed. F. L. Lucas (London, 1927), I, 135.

39. *Ibid.*, p. 191.

40. *Ibid.*, p. 145.

41. *Ibid.*, p. 160.

42. *Ibid.*, p. 154.

43. *Ibid.*, II, 41.

44. John Ford, *Selected Plays*, ed. Havelock Ellis (London, 1888), p. 31.

45. Wells, *op. cit.*

46. All references to the text of Shakespeare are to the edition of G. L. Kittredge (Boston, 1936).

47. Mark Van Doren, *Shakespeare* (New York, 1939), p. 105.

48. *Ibid.*, p. 104.

49. George Orwell, "The Art of Donald McGill," in *Dickens, Dali and Others* (New York, 1946), p. 136.

50. Rylands, *op. cit.*, pp. 147, 148.

51. Van Doren, *op. cit.*, p. 116.

52. Sharpe, *op. cit.*, p. 558.

53. C. E. Montague, "Shakspere's Way With Agincourt," in *Dramatic Values* (London, 1931; originally published 1910), pp. 170, 171.

54. O. J. Campbell, in *Comicall Satyre and Shakespeare's 'Troilus and Cressida'* (San Marino, Calif., 1938), has convincingly demonstrated the probable influence of the satirical dramatic form on Shakespeare's play.

55. "Shakespeare's Prose", *Overland Monthly*, XV, (San Francisco, 1875), 506–514.

56. Van Doren, *op. cit.*, p. 197 *et seq.*

57. *The Works of John Marston*, ed. A. H. Bullen (London, 1888), I, 220.

58. Harley Granville-Barker, "King Lear," in *Prefaces to Shakespeare*, I (Princeton, 1946), 278, 279.

59. *Ibid.*, p. 294.

60. *The Complete Works of Shakespeare*, ed. G. L. Kittredge (Boston, 1936), p. 1045.

61. Harley Granville-Barker, "Antony and Cleopatra," in *Prefaces to Shakespeare*, I (Princeton, 1946), 418.

62. George Philip Krapp, *The Rise of English Literary Prose* (New York, 1915), pp. 457ff.

63. J. H. Francis, *From Caxton to Carlyle* (Cambridge, 1937), p. 71.

64. Van Doren, *op. cit.*, p. 128.

65. J. Dover Wilson, *The Manuscript of Shakespeare's Hamlet* (Cambridge, 1934), II, 50.

66. E. K. Chambers, *William Shakespeare* (Oxford, 1930), I, 183.

67. "The Copy for the Text of 1623," in *As You Like It*, ed. Arthur Quiller-Couch and J. Dover Wilson (Cambridge, 1926).

68. *Ibid.*, p. 94.

69. *Idem.*

70. *Ibid.*, pp. 94, 95.

71. *Ibid.*, p. 95.

72. *Ibid.*, p. 129.

73. *Ibid.*, p. 148.

74. *The Tempest*, ed. Arthur Quiller-Couch and J. Dover Wilson (Cambridge, 1921).

75. *The Two Gentlemen of Verona*, ed. Arthur Quiller-Couch and J. Dover Wilson (Cambridge, 1921).

76. *Measure for Measure*, ed. Arthur Quiller-Couch and J. Dover Wilson (Cambridge, 1922).

77. *Ben Jonson, Selected Works*, ed. Harry Levin (New York, 1938), p. 1001.

BIBLIOGRAPHY

I. *Texts*

Beaumont, Francis, and Fletcher, John, *Selected Plays*, ed. J. St. Loe Strachey, 2 vol. (London, 1887).

Chapman, George, *The Plays and Poems of George Chapman*, ed. T. M. Parrott, 3 vol. (London, 1914).

Dekker, Thomas, *Selected Plays*, ed. Ernest Rhys (London, 1894).

Ford, John, *Selected Plays*, ed. Havelock Ellis (London, 1888).

Greene, Robert, *The Plays and Poems of Robert Greene*, ed. J. Churton Collins, 2 vol. (Oxford, 1905).

Heywood, Thomas, *Selected Plays*, ed. A. W. Verity (London, 1888).

Jonson, Ben, *Ben Jonson*, ed. C. H. Herford and Percy Simpson, (London, 1925).

— *Ben Jonson, Selected Works*, ed. Harry Levin (New York, 1938).

— *The Works of Ben Jonson*, ed. Brinsley Nicholson and C. H. Herford, 3 vol. (London, 1893–95).

Kyd, Thomas, *The Works of Thomas Kyd*, ed. F. S. Boas (Oxford, 1901).

Marlowe, Christopher, *The Works of Christopher Marlowe*, ed. C. F. Tucker Brooke (Oxford, 1910).

— *The Tragical History of Doctor Faustus*, ed. F. S. Boas (London, 1932).

Marston, John, *The Works of John Marston*, ed. A. H. Bullen, 3 vol. (London, 1888).

Middleton, Thomas, *Selected Plays*, ed. Havelock Ellis, 2 vol. (London, 1890).

Peele, George, *The Works of George Peele*, ed. A. H. Bullen, 2 vol. (London, 1888).

Shakespeare, William, *The Complete Works of Shakespeare*, ed. G. L. Kittredge (Boston, 1936).

— *As You Like It*, ed. Arthur Quiller-Couch and J. Dover Wilson (Cambridge, 1926).

— *Measure for Measure*, ed. Arthur Quiller-Couch and J. Dover Wilson (Cambridge, 1922).

— *The Tempest*, ed. Arthur Quiller-Couch and J. Dover Wilson (Cambridge, 1921).

— *The Two Gentlemen of Verona*, ed. Sir Arthur Quiller-Couch and J. Dover Wilson (Cambridge, 1921).

Shirley, James, *Selected Plays*, ed. Edmund Gosse (London, 1888).

Tourneur, Cyril, *The Plays of Webster and Tourneur*, ed. J. A. Symonds (London, 1888).

Webster, John, *The Complete Works of John Webster*, ed. F. L. Lucas, 4 vol. (London, 1927).

II. *Criticism (general)*

Bradley, A. C., *Shakespearean Tragedy* (London, 1904).

Campbell, O. J., *Comicall Satyre and Shakespeare's 'Troilus and Cressida'* (San Marino, Calif., 1938).

Chambers, E. K., *William Shakespeare*, 2 vol. (Oxford, 1930).

Francis, J. H., *From Caxton to Carlyle* (Cambridge, 1937).

Krapp, George Philip, *The Rise of English Literary Prose* (New York, 1915).

Montague, C. E., "Shakspere's Way With Agincourt," in *Dramatic Values* (London, 1931; originally published 1910).

Orwell, George, "The Art of Donald McGill," in *Dickens, Dali and Others* (New York, 1946).

Simpson, Percy, "The 1604 Text of Marlowe's 'Dr. Faustus,' *Essays and Studies by Members of the English Association*, VII (Oxford, 1921), 143–155.

— "Marlowe's 'Tragical History of Dr. Faustus,'" *Essays and Studies by Members of the English Association*, XIV (Oxford, 1929), 20–34.

Van Doren, Mark, *Shakespeare* (New York, 1939).

Wilson, J. Dover, *The Manuscript of Shakespeare's Hamlet*, 2 vol. (Cambridge, 1934).

III. *Criticism (special studies)*

Bordukat, Gertrud, *Die Abgrenzung zwischen Vers und Prosa in den Dramen Shakespeares*, Diss. (Königsberg, 1918).
Distinguishes four types of prose in Shakespeare: comic prose, used chiefly by fools and the lower classes; humorous or witty prose used by the upper classes; ordinary serious prose of the lower classes; "finer" serious prose of the upper classes.

Collins, J. Churton, "Shakespeare as a Prose Writer," in *Studies in Shakespeare* (London, 1904), pp. 180–208.
Distinguishes five "styles" of Shakespeare's prose: "The euphuistic... the coarse colloquial prose, modelled on the language of vulgar life... the prose of higher comedy... prose professedly rhetorical... highly wrought poetical prose."

Corson, Hiram, *An Introduction to the Study of Shakespeare* (Boston, 1889).
Shakespeare uses prose for "all the dramatis personæ that are not drawn into the higher movements of thought or feeling."

David, Richard, *The Janus of Poets* (London, 1935).
"The chief purpose of [Shakespeare's] prose is.... to provide.... the strongest possible contrast to the staple verse."

Delius, Nicolaus, "Die Prosa in Shakespere's Dramen," in *Abhandlungen zu Shakespere* (Elberfeld, 1878), reprinted from *Jahrbuch der deutschen Shakespeare-Gesellschaft* (1870).
Recognizes three chief "styles": clown-prose, the prose used in conversation by educated people of some social standing, and Euphuistic prose.

Granville-Barker, Harley, *Prefaces to Shakespeare*, 2 vol. (Princeton, 1946–47).
The essays on *King Lear* and *Antony and Cleopatra* are especially suggestive about the implications of Shakespeare's uses of prose for the most effective understanding and presentation of the plays in the theatre.

Janssen, V. F., *Die Prosa in Shakespeares Dramen*, Diss. (Straßburg, 1897).
Lists twelve categories of the uses of prose, on no discernible principle.

Klein, Magdalene, "Shakespeares Dramatisches Formgesetz," *Wortkunst*, Neue Folge, 4. Heft (München, 1930).
Explains the use of prose and verse in Shakespeare's plays in terms of an opposition between tension (*Spannung*) and release (*Lockerung*), verse being used for tension and prose for release.

Macdonald, J. F. "The Use of Prose in English Drama Before Shakespeare," *University of Toronto Quarterly*, II, 4 (Toronto, July, 1933), 465–481.
Distinguishes four prime uses of prose: for letters, formal documents or proclamations, mad scenes, and comic scenes; and two secondary uses: "the regular speech of the clowns, rustics, and

lower characters in general, especially in comedy" and "the regular speech in ordinary commercial business."

Mégroz, R. L., *Shakespeare as a Letter-Writer and Artist in Prose* (London, 1927).
Two anthologies, one of Shakespeare's letters, the other of prose passages not including letters; and a "disquisition" (sic), commending Henry Sharpe's list of rules for the use of prose in Shakespeare's plays (which see below).

Muncaster, Mary, "The Use of Prose in Elizabethan Drama," *Modern Language Review*, XIV (Cambridge, 1919), 10–15.
In pre-Shakespearean drama, the use of prose or verse is determined largely by the social class of the speaker; in later Elizabethan drama, the use of prose is determined by: 1) character; 2) action, i. e., characters involved in dramatic action speak verse, others prose; 3) "Stimmung"—the "mood" of a scene; and 4) conventional usages.

Romig, Edna Davis, "Shakespeare's Prose," *University of Colorado Studies*, XV, 1 (1925), 75–94.
A summary of some of the earlier studies.

Rylands, George H. W., *Words and Poetry* (London, 1928).
Considers Shakespeare's use of prose important for the light it sheds on the development of his mature verse style; the prose represents, in Shakespeare, "a reaction against the diction and versification of the day" and "character and dramatic realism breaking through fashions and conventions."

Sharpe, Henry, "The Prose in Shakspere's Plays," *Transactions of the New Shakspere Society*, Series 1, No. 10 (1880–86), pp. 523–562.
Offers a list of fourteen general and five special rules for the use of prose and verse in Shakespeare's plays, all based chiefly on character. (Example: "Poor men speak prose... messengers speak metre.")

Sill, Edward Rowland, "Shakespeare's Prose," *Overland Monthly*, XV (San Francisco, 1875), 523–562.
A study of the use of prose in *Hamlet*, suggesting that verse is used to denote sincerity and prose insincerity on the part of the speaker.

Wells, Henry W., "The Continuity of Shaksperian Prose," *Shakespeare Association Bulletin*, XV, 3 (July, 1940), 175–183.
Argues that Shakespeare's prose is fully mature from the very beginning of Shakespeare's career, whereas the verse constantly develops.

INDEX